20 First Dates

20 First Dates

My Search for Mr Right

Rebecca K. Maddox

18 17 16 15 14 13 12 7 6 5 4 3 2 1

First published 2011 by Authentic Media Limited
52 Presley Way, Crownhill, Milton Keynes, MK8 0ES
www.authenticmedia.co.uk

British Library Cataloguing in Publication Data

A catalogue record for this book is available from the British Library

ISBN-13: 978-1-85078-991-8

All names have been changed to protect the identity of the people involved

Cover design by David Smart
Printed and bound by CPI Group (UK) Ltd., Croydon, CR0 4YY

To Adam – my last man

CONTENTS

Introduction

Hi there. My name is Becky and I am a single Christian woman of 28 years, who feels ready to meet my life partner. My church friends and family know I am ready; my non-church friends and family also know; above all else, God knows. And yet nothing is happening. So, despite a history of spectacular (and often hilarious) failure in this field I decided that I would not give up. In fact, I would do the opposite, and make myself an expert in dating. How would I do this? Well, as an experiment, I would go on twenty dates with twenty different men who I found in twenty different ways; then write up my research.

Some people I spoke to about this were very excited. They jumped up and down, laughed, clapped their hands at the prospect. Others were not so convinced. Some people told me to 'wait on God' or to 'follow Jesus and all this will be added to you'. This seemed true at first glance – there is a simplicity to it, a patience. I have even told it to myself in the past once in a while. But truthfully it wasn't working for me, and it just isn't working for a lot of people.

I look around my church and there is so clearly an issue. My friend Marion is intelligent, funny, beautiful, kind and . . . single. We both know she'd rather not be single, but she's just waiting patiently. Then there's my friend Neil – again the same story: good-looking guy, sweet, funny. Why is he on his own?

Could it be because of the 'wait and see' philosophy advocated by some churches? The idea that we just need to wait patiently and a spouse will plop into our laps – probably when we are sitting praying in church one day! The 'wait and see' approach is based on the idea that God is like lightning – he strikes, and something amazing happens to us – a new dream job, the perfect partner. But in reality God doesn't work like that – striking without any counter-effort, and I recently discovered that neither does lightning. When a bolt of lightning strikes, the bolt doesn't actually reach down from the heavens and touch the ground. The downwards electrical charge only reaches to about the height of a very tall tree. Then a counter-charge comes up from the ground to meet the electricity from the sky, and a lightning bolt is formed, with the illusion that the ground is being struck from above.

Our interactions with God are exactly the same. We can't just sit around waiting for him to do something – we have to act too. So if you were hoping for a new job, you would pray of course, but you would also improve your CV, read the job adverts, apply, go through the merry-go-round of interviews, until you got the right job for you. God's input is essential, but you wouldn't just sit around at home waiting for a job to fall out of the sky into your lap. At least, hopefully you wouldn't! So if we Christians wouldn't take this approach to finding a job, why on earth are we trying to find husbands and wives in this way?! It is as though we are super-spiritualizing the whole thing; paralysing ourselves with fear, and failing to get anywhere as a result.

After I heard about the fact that lightning strikes up as well as down, I couldn't shake the feeling that God wants us to be active participants in finding our soul mate. It is *exactly* the same with relationships as with jobs. Pray, but also seek, knock, search and (hopefully) find. My argument is that we should acknowledge that God is in control, but play our part too. This book, and the research that went into it, is my way of taking action and trusting God in the process.

I was on the verge of giving up at the time I started this endeavour, but I was willing to take a few more steps in the world of Christian dating because I want to encourage you that it can be done, it should be done, and if it ends in embarrassment with egg down your trousers then it's not the end of the world. Eventually it will work out.

Ultimately, what we all want to see is God's will done on earth – and we are the hands, feet and hearts that can do this – in all sorts of ways, including loving one another.

I hope you enjoy reading about my adventures, and that they encourage you to have some of your own. Happy reading!

Becky

Author's Note

When I started writing this book I was planning to just describe my dating experiences and leave it at that. But as I read around the subject and spoke to friends I realized that dating is not a straightforward subject for many Christians. There is no template or blueprint as to how you should go about wooing in the Bible (except for some hints in Song of Songs and Ruth). Some people question whether it is advisable for Christians to do the dating thing at all, and even for those who think it is fine there are some potential risky areas. Then there is the question of whether you are personally ready to face the probable mistakes and knock-backs of the search. These days you can't just curl up at the feet of your kinsman-redeemer and be married soon after, as Ruth was. It is all a lot more complicated for us modern day girls and guys.

I felt all these issues needed to be addressed, and so this book covers a lot of ground. I hope that by the time you get to the end you will have no excuse whatsoever for not getting out there and getting dating!

PART I

THE DATES

In which some of the highlights and low points of my twenty dates are described, along with some practical suggestions for your own dating adventures

1

ICE CREAM AND FALLING PIGEONS

OR 'THE WORST DATE I HAVE EVER HAD, EVER'

'If you can meet with triumph or disaster,
And treat those two imposters just the same'
– Rudyard Kipling

About a year and a half ago, I had an experience that sparked off my desire to write this book. I was a member of a small group at my church. We were all single women, but we didn't make too much of a big deal out of it (though it was a big deal really if we were honest). Sometimes we did activities directly relating to our 'single woman walk'. One evening we went to a talk about singleness and marriage by a Specialist – note the capital 'S'! She had just written a book, so we thought that she might have a few tips.

We went to the talk that Friday evening with hope and expectation in our hearts, bright-eyed and eager to hear some words of wisdom from a mature Christian lady. The optimistic part of me hoped that we'd all be paired up with suitable men by the end of the evening, and we would go home happy, with that part of our lives sorted out.

We got to the hall, did some worship – so far, so good. Then the Specialist arrived on stage. We sat up eagerly in our chairs, ready to receive some wisdom. But as the lady began speaking I could see my friends shrinking in their chairs – turning from alert, eager Christian women, all bright eyes and wet noses – into cowed and visibly shrivelled shadows of what they once were. The essential message of this lady's harangue was that it was our own fault we were single and we all needed to get our acts together – we had to get out there and grab our soul mates by the throat, shake some sense into them and get hitched. It was more than a little alarming. As the Specialist strode about the stage shouting, my heart sank lower and lower. One of her main arguments seemed to be that she was married, so why couldn't the rest of us manage it? I have to say, this was one point I could agree with. So, by the end of the evening, we were all exhausted and not one of us was any closer to finding our soulmate.

Or were we . . .?

Perhaps there was a chance of something good coming from this evening after all . . .

At the very last minute hope was rekindled in the form of a pleasant looking chap called Richard.

Richard had clearly taken the 'go-getter' message of the evening to heart. Emboldened, he said hello –and asked for my number just as we walked out of the door. It certainly perked me up, and I gleefully (but subtly) exchanged numbers with him. (I tried to do it subtly as I didn't want the others mocking me, and couldn't help feeling a bit bad that they hadn't got numbers too – unless they, too, were being subtle about their own conquests!) Have you ever tried to be simultaneously subtle and gleeful about something? It's a great feeling, like the feeling you get the day before your birthday as a kid.

So, Richard and I met again three days later in a well-known pizza restaurant (the not-so-up-market one), where we ate pizza, drank watery fizzy pop and chased it all down with an 'ice cream factory'.

You fill a bowl with Mr Whippy soft ice cream and then add as much sauce and as many toppings as you want

I don't know if you have ever experienced an 'ice cream factory', but it is not an easy thing to have to deal with when you are trying to appear attractive to a member of the opposite sex. When you choose the 'ice cream factory', you fill a bowl with Mr Whippy soft ice cream and then add as much sauce and as many toppings as you want. You can go back and do it again as many times as you want during the evening.

It sounds like heaven, and on any normal day, it would be. But not on date night. As soon as we ordered it, I realised it was a bad idea. But there was no going back.

We stood in line with our little plastic bowls and I got increasingly nervous as the small children in front of us screamed and fought over the last chocolate button. When we at last reached the front, Richard filled his bowl with a modest amount of ice cream and decorated it skilfully with just enough chocolate sauce and marshmallows. He looked like a pro, even flicking the top of his ice cream into a neat little swirl. Phew – a hard act to follow! Nervously I stepped up with my bowl, and turned on the machine. Soft coils of ice cream fell into the bowl, twisting round in a very satisfying way. Maybe this wasn't so bad! I watched the ice cream coils fall; the bowl filling gradually, the machine swirling. And then it was full. Time to turn off the machine.

Problem.

I couldn't figure out how to make it stop. I tried twisting the nozzle, pressing it, squeezing it, but nothing worked – the ice cream kept coming and it wouldn't stop. It was like one of those films where a giant plant grows and takes over a whole city. Just like a killer-plant, the ice cream took over my bowl completely, and soon it was snaking on to the floor as well. Just as it looked like the ice cream was going to take over the whole restaurant, Richard came to my rescue, and flicked the off switch. I looked up, gasping, 'Thank you!' Sheepishly we both moved away from the scene of the crime.

Back at the table the mountain of plain ice cream towered between us (I had been too embarrassed to hang around decorating it). The monstrous pudding impeded our view of one another and also threatened imminent collapse at any moment. I began to excavate desperately, eating as fast as I could. But it was a warm restaurant and I simply couldn't keep up with the forces of nature. Slowly, inexorably, the pile of ice cream slumped to the side and then onto the table where it formed a small pool that began spreading out gradually across the tablecloth.

'Don't worry about it.' Richard smiled at me, and I smiled back with my head full of sugar, wondering if this could be love.

Mud and bird flu

The ice cream factory incident didn't seem to have put Richard off and, the next Saturday, we met up again. This time we drove to a nearby village for a cosy pub lunch. Well, maybe it was the lack of an ice cream factory to get things going, but it didn't go too well over lunch. On that damp Saturday afternoon we began to run out of conversation.

The date went from bad to worse after lunch. I tried to interest him in the ducks puddling around in the muddy pond, pointing and leaping about, doing an impression of one of the ducks. But comedy ducks were clearly not one of his interests. Over lunch I had told him that I was a keen walker, so we decided to go for a walk. As we walked and talked, I'm sorry to say that our common ground dwindled. He professed an interest in music. I said I enjoyed music too. Nothing. I tried to tell him about my overseas trips. He said he had been abroad a few times as well. Then, nothing. It seemed like nothing was going to work, and a dull boredom set in.

It was as we trudged around the border of a muddy field that the lowest point was reached. It had been raining and the path was really muddy. I looked at it carefully, and judged it to be OK – took a confident step, slipped and fell on my bum. It was not graceful – minus points for femininity. I stood up with a brave smile, half covered in mud but determined to carry on regardless. But no sooner had I got up than – wump! I was on my bottom again.

It was no good. Walking upright was impossible. I had not brought walking boots and my shoes had no grip – I was sliding all over the place. There was no other option. I had to hold Richard's hand in order to make it down the path. It was awkward. I didn't really feel like holding his hand, and he had to contend with a mud-monster so I don't suppose he was too keen either. When he grabbed my hand there was no Beatles tribute

I looked at it carefully, and judged it to be OK – took a confident step, slipped and fell on my bum

band singing 'I wanna hold your hand', there were no warm fuzzy feelings, no light-headedness, just a grim determination to get to the other side of the sea of mud.

It was then that things went from bad to downright strange.

A pigeon fell out of the sky.

Right in front of us.

Richard and I let go of each other's hands in surprise. We both looked at the pigeon.

It was dead.

We both looked up into the sky to see where it had come from.

The sky was clear.

We looked down at the pigeon again.

We must have looked hilarious to God at that moment. Like a couple of nodding dogs in a field, one covered with mud.

We were completely flummoxed. There were no trees or shrubbery or pigeon hiding places. It must have simply been flying and dropped dead. Maybe of a heart attack. Or bird flu. Or mad pigeon syndrome. Who knows?

At that point we stopped looking at the pigeon and the sky because it started raining, and we decided it was definitely time to go home.

Back in the car park we encountered another problem. The car wouldn't start. We sat for nearly an hour trying to make it go. I'm afraid at this point I did something rather dishonourable. I called a taxi and went home, leaving Richard to sort out the car. I did have a prior appointment, but I still felt bad as the taxi drove off.

Fortunately I received a text message ten minutes later saying that the car's engine had mysteriously sprung into life almost as soon as I left.

Richard and I never made contact again.

And we never did find out why that pigeon fell from the sky.

❖ ❖ ❖

On the face of it this date looks like a disaster, and in many ways perhaps it was. But I would actually see it as a success, because at least we tested the water and found out that we were not suited.

No harm done, no bones broken. No dignity permanently lost, just temporarily mislaid.

(I exclude the pigeon from this summary. Sadly, he permanently lost everything on that day.)

So it turns out that the lady who gave the talk was right. We do have to get our acts together. It is better to go for it and test the water than never to know. I'm glad Richard suggested we swap numbers, even though it didn't work out. At least we tried. Wouldn't it be great if you could get a guaranteed embarrassing date at every Christian singles event you went to? Let's make it happen!

I'm glad that Richard was bold enough to ask me out and get things going with the dates. I understand from Facebook that he has now met the woman of his dreams and is soon to marry her; which shows that his attitude paid off in the end. Well done, Richard. And as for me, well after the pigeon date I was ready for anything. It was time to start searching for men to date!

2

PLENTY OF FISH IN THE SEA?
(WHERE TO FIND YOUR DATES PART I)

'My heart is a lonely hunter that hunts on a lonely hill'
– Fiona McLeod, 1855–1905

So I left the disaster of the pigeon date behind and embarked on my adventure of finding nineteen more men to date. The first important question to address was where to find all my willing dates. I decided to make a list of all the ways to meet men that I could think of.

Here is the list, which I more or less stuck to over the next few months, and which you can try working your way through too if you are so inclined. Some of them are quite random, others more obvious. I wanted to be a bit daring and try lots of different things:

1) Look in my own church
2) 'Flirt to convert'
3) In a Christian bookshop
4) Look in another church
5) At a wedding
6) Elders' recommendation
7) Friends' recommendation
8) Dating website

9) Searching Facebook
10) Speed dating
11) Singles party
12) Christian holiday or day away
13) Conference
14) Christian summer festival
15) Through work
16) Double date with an established couple
17) Shared interest dating – take up a new hobby
18) Take out a personal ad
19) In the pub after church
20) Through sheer cheek and opportunism

It is worth mentioning that some of these methods produced a lovely date (or even more than one lovely date!), others produced a lousy date, and some produced no date at all!

Anyway, I decided it made sense to start local . . .

Fishing in your own pond?

It might seem like your church is the obvious place to start when looking for a partner, and in many ways it is. A person from your own church is likely to share your values and outlook on faith. They are likely to be part of the same friendship groups already, which saves you a lot of troublesome introductions. Crucially they are also likely to live near you, which is not only convenient, but is often essential for love to develop fully.

However, I was once advised by a friend not to go 'fishing in my own pond'. This is quite wise in some ways because if you go fishing for a mate in your own church and you land a 'tiddler' you can't gently put him back without everyone noticing. Alternatively, you

I was once advised by a friend not to go 'fishing in my own pond'

might land a scorpion fish, which is much more dangerous and spectacular. Do you really want to provide a side-show for your church friends and family, as you attempt to disentangle an unwanted fish from your line? Probably not.

A few of my twenty dates were within the home pond, but none of them worked out.

It has to be said that there are certain dangers in dating at your home church. Leaving aside stretched metaphors of shark-infested waters and 'swimming upstream', there is a tendency for church to be a place of gossip and speculation. Even with the best of intentions from your church family, you can feel under the microscope. This doesn't mean that you shouldn't go for it if there is a potential soul mate at your particular church; but on the whole it's unlikely that you will meet your partner there, especially if you belong to a small church, or one that is particularly couple-heavy or family-orientated.

So in a world where we are all looking for the fish equivalent of a sleek salmon to date, where should we look?

There are plenty of other opportunities for Christians to meet other Christians out there. Which is why my next choice of method was slightly odd and ultimately unsuccessful . . .

Flirt to convert?

It all went wrong at the work Christmas curry party.

The evening was going well. We're great friends at my work. It is like a big family, with the inevitable tiffs and rifts – but on the whole we get on. So there we were, waiting for our starters, and conversation turned to this book, which I was starting to research. I had only had one date so far and the prospect of getting nineteen more was daunting. So my colleagues were helpfully making suggestions about how to get dates, who the dates should be, what I should wear, what I should say and so on. In fact they were planning every detail of all twenty dates pretty much, but anyway . . .

As we were eating and chatting, another group came into the restaurant and they were nearly all men. There were about thirty of them, accompanied by just five women. Thirty good-looking young men with a maximum of five taken ones! Surely I'd be able to find my next date among that lot? Egged on by my colleagues I struck up a conversation with one. We discovered that they were part of the Territorial Army. Interesting – that explained why they were so male-heavy. I don't really see myself with an army man, but such was the tone of the evening's conversation that I felt I ought to be open to any possibility. So I picked out one in a long-sleeved grey T-shirt who looked quite cute.

'Go on – ask him out,' said Jess. 'He could be the next date.'

'You ask him if he's a Christian first,' I said.

'No, no – it's flirt to convert, not convert to flirt – ask him out!'

Eventually I had to get up to go to the loo. There was only one ladies loo,

So I picked out one in a long-sleeved grey T-shirt who looked quite cute

and it was occupied so I waited. Then who should walk through the door but grey-T-shirt man. It was nothing less than I sign from God. It had to be.

'Hello,' I said, in a breezy, cheerful and non-threatening way.

'Hello,' he replied, slightly nervously.

'Are you a Christian?' (Being rather flustered, I had forgotten to flirt first and commit later.)

'Er, no. Well – yes. But I'm not practising.'

'You don't need to practise really,' I blurted. 'You just are a Christian – you become it. You can't get good at it by practising.' I was blabbering now – reaching that stage where I thought that keeping on talking was a good plan, when it clearly was not.

He smiled in a polite but perplexed way then disappeared into the men's toilet, leaving me to ponder the oddness of what I had just said.

A 'practising Christian'. I do find this phrase very strange when I actually think about it. You don't practise your relationship with God. It's not a rehearsal. It's a living thing that you work at and act out day by day. You never know what to expect, what God is going to give you and how you will deal with it. You can't practise. But in other ways I suppose you are practising all the time. You are choosing to read your Bible, go to church, not follow through on a certain thought. You are forming habits of mind, training yourself up for the kingdom. You are disciplining and disciple-ing yourself – which does take practice.

I surfaced from my reverie . . .

Whoever was in the ladies toilet was taking an awfully long time; so long in fact that grey-T-shirt man finished in the men's and reappeared. I decided I might as well pick up the conversation where it left off . . . perhaps ill-advisedly, but still . . .

'I just asked about the Christian thing because I'm writing a book about Christian dating you see . . .' I began in as nonchalant a way as I could manage. 'So if you were a Christian I was going to ask you out . . . but you're not.'

The man laughed nervously. It must have seemed quite strange to him, to find this woman still hanging about outside the loo. 'No – well, shame, eh? But there you go.'

'There you go,' I laughed back, equally nervously.

And there *he* went – out of the loos and back to his table.

As I walked back into the restaurant after finally getting into the ladies, I began to wish that I had put on more make-up as a disguise. Everyone on grey-T-shirt man's table was looking at me, staring and pointing. Well, they probably weren't actually pointing, but in my mind they were.

I went back to the table and told my colleagues the sorry story of the 'conversation'. It didn't get the reaction I expected:

'He went to the toilet after you – it's a sign. God meant you to talk to him.'

'You should ask him out – he's a sort-of Christian after all.'

'His eternal salvation might depend on you!'

In retrospect they were clearly winding me up, having had one too many Cobra beers, but at the time I thought they were serious. Feeling the weighty responsibility of the last comment, I was persuaded

'He went to the toilet after you – it's a sign. God meant you to talk to him'

to write my number on a scrap of paper to give to him. Someone suggested I write 'God loves you' as well, but I thought this would be weird, so just stuck with the number and my name.

I was feeling fine, confident. I had my paper ready – my phone number on the back of a butcher's receipt given to me by my colleague. ('Chicken and bacon pie £5.20; Pork pie £1.30; Sausages £2.20.' What if grey-T-shirt man was a vegetarian, I wondered?) Anyway, veggie or not I was going to go for it.

Then my chance came. He was leaving. This was it. I had to do it. Now.

Jess hissed, 'Go on!'

I half-rose from my chair as he walked towards the door.

I tapped him on the shoulder.

He kept walking.

I tapped again, saying, 'Excuse me.'

He kept walking.

I had to get up from my seat and tug the sleeve of his jacket to get him to turn round. Relief washing over me, I handed him the scrap of paper and smiled sweetly: 'Just in case,' I said. He looked perplexed and muttered, 'Thanks.'

I turned round to see all my colleagues staring at me, aghast. It was a horrible moment as I realized that the whole thing – my struggle to gain his attention, my awkward little 'excuse me', the way I stumbled over a chair leg – every detail had been witnessed by all my work colleagues, including my boss, the head of the company.

And to make it worse, it turned out that the man in the grey T-shirt wasn't actually leaving at all – he was just going out for a cigarette. I had to spend the rest of the evening trying not to look over at him.

So don't go for the option of trying to find your next date at a work's Christmas curry evening – even if you work for a Christian organization like I do. And don't choose an agnostic, chain-smoking member of the TA who you talk to in the toilet queue.

A few days later grey-T-shirt man texted me: 'Am not up for a relationship, but how about a bit of fun?' Hmm, not so good – I didn't reply and deleted him from my phone.

No more flirting to convert I decided – it just didn't seem to work! Although I do still wonder whether grey-T-shirt man went back to church as a result. Very doubtful, but you never know . . .

Bookworm love

After the flirt-to-convert experience, I wanted to try something where I could be sure of the Christian credentials of the man in question . . . What could be better than the sober, calm and thoughtful atmosphere of a Christian bookshop?

Surely this was a fail-safe way of picking up an earnest Christian man? The idea was that I would hang around my local Christian bookshop and wait for all the hot, slightly geeky, single, Christian men to come in, see me, fall instantly and permanently in love and ask me to marry them. I thought I was onto a winner. The men would be clever and interesting because they were in a bookshop, and Christian because . . . well do I really need to explain? Plus I could be sure we would have at least one interest in common before we even got talking – books – fail safe!

Well, after half an hour of standing around 'browsing' I was not doing particularly well. Only three men had entered the shop and none of them had looked remotely eligible. They were all well over 50. The only one who looked slightly closer in age to me was pushing a pram and had gold glinting on his wedding ring finger.

I was looking at it mostly because the author photo on the front was a cute young American man

Incidentally, I can tell you that I became quite used to looking out for that tell-tale golden glint over the next few months. In fact, if you're searching for a husband or wife I would recommend looking at someone's finger before you even say 'hello'. It saves an awful lot of embarrassment and time.

Anyway, as I stood there, I began to wonder whether maybe all the hot, single Christian men did their Christian book shopping on a Friday, rather than on a Saturday afternoon. There was certainly a lack of them in this particular Christian bookshop. I was just looking at the cover of a particularly earnest looking book about staying away from the dating scene – if I'm honest I was looking at it mostly because the author photo on the front was a cute young American man – when I became aware of someone nearby. I looked up and there was a man next to me nonchalantly perusing the 'relationships and lifestlye' section of the store – good looking, in that geek-chic way, with glasses and fluffy hair. He looked about 35. I glanced down at his hand – no wedding ring! This was it . . . a date, surely?

'Excuse me, have you read this?' I showed him the cover of the book in my hands, giving my sweetest smile.

He looked at the book, then looked at me; brow furrowed.

'Yes, yes I have,' he replied, making as if to turn away . . .

'Is it any good?' I asked eagerly, forcing him to engage.

'Excellent. Yes.' The man regarded me suspiciously through his glasses. 'The author makes a very good case for not dating at all; for waiting for God's timing. I have to say I totally agree.'

There was a momentary pause as I digested this information.

'Oh, OK.' I smiled again. 'So are you buying anything?'

'No.' The man pressed his lips together, turned and headed towards the door.

'Well, nice to meet you,' I called out to his receding form.

He glanced back at me with a worried frown-smile and exited the shop.

I sighed and looked down at the book in my hands with its smug and handsome cover-star. He smirked at me. 'Looks like you're my date for the evening then,' I thought grumpily inside my head. I walked over to the till, put the book on the counter and got out my purse. The grey-haired lady gave a sardonic smile as I put my debit card on the counter and turned her eyes in the direction of the door, with a slight lift of her eyebrows. I smiled sheepishly and shrugged as I made my payment.

So instead of going on a date that evening I read the book, disagreed with most of it, reluctantly agreed with some of it, and decided it was aimed at teenagers rather than adults in their thirties.

Even now when I think about the cute, bookish guy I think it's a shame. But there we are. You can't believe everything you read.

No quitting!

These were my first few tentative steps into the world of intentional Christian dating. They didn't work particularly well for me, but they might for you. As it was, I was only just warming up, and there was a lot more yet to come . . . So, unperturbed by these experiences, I decided to press on to the next stage. It was time to shop around. It was time to start church-visiting.

3

OTHER PEOPLE'S PONDS AND TREE CATHEDRALS (WHERE TO FIND YOUR DATES PART II)

'If the mountain will not come to Mahomet,
Mahomet must go to the mountain'

After the bad experience of fishing for men in my home church pond; I began to wonder about the untapped potential within the walls of all the other churches out there. There are 47,500 churches in the UK. Surely one of those had to hold my Mr Right – or at least a date!

Gone fishing

So it was that Megan, Sarah, Linda, Lisa and I found ourselves squashed into Megan's small car, driving through the Home Counties towards the outskirts of London on a dark winter's night to seek out new life and new civilizations, to boldly go where no woman had gone before. We were going on a man hunt in another church!

We decided on this particular church because Megan had been invited by a man she met on the Internet. Megan actually wanted to meet this man, but she also wanted some protection in case he was a weirdo. Plus, we all wanted an evening away from our usual church and the chance to scout out some men too. So this was a win-win situation for all involved (not least the unsuspecting men of the London church that we were aiming for, of course!).

We chatted and laughed as we drove – and yes, the subject of men did come up once or twice.

We covered the important topic of over-enthusiasm in the Christian dating scene; and agreed that an invitation to go for a coffee does not mean marriage, babies and happily-ever-after as many people seem to think it does. We were unanimously agreed that anyone who approaches a date with this in mind is crazy – whether they are a man or a woman.

Megan then told a story about a 'Fire and Ice' singles party she had been to where guests were given a sheet of paper with boxes to tick and you had to find the person who ticked all your boxes. I thought Megan said 'tickled your boxers', which was slightly alarming.

It was a very dark night and we were running late, so Megan was speeding somewhat. We were confidently following the satnav, racing along, enjoying the conversation, and then later singing along to worship music at the top of our voices. As we drove it got darker and darker; and we suddenly realized that we were on a road with no street lights; then a country road, then an unmade dirt track, until finally we could go no further.

'In 200 yards you will reach your destination,' said the sugary American satnav voice

'In 200 yards you will reach your destination,' said the sugary American satnav voice.

Our 'destination' was a metal-barred gate blocking

the way, with a National Trust sign hanging off it and a potato field beyond. The car screeched to a halt.

'You have reached your destination,' said the smooth voice.

Megan looked around – taking in as much of the scene as could be made out in the beam of the headlights.

'You have reached your destination,' repeated the voice, insistently.

'No, we haven't!' yelled Megan in frustration.

'Hey – wait a minute,' said Linda, 'maybe this is our destination. Maybe this guy is a complete nutcase, and he's lured you to this secluded spot in order to attack you.'

'Yeah – maybe,' breathed Sarah.

'Thank goodness you guys are here with me.' Megan looked round, straining to see anything. 'Hey! – maybe that's the place.'

She pointed, and we all looked to see what she was pointing at.

It was a lonely farmhouse about a mile away, with a pale glow in one of the ground-floor windows indicating someone was at home.

'Hmm . . . Well that's not a church,' deduced Lisa.

'Probably an axe murderer's house,' I added, really unhelpfully.

'Maybe I should get out and have a look,' said Megan, starting to open the door.

But Sarah was getting twitchy. 'No – let's get out of here, I'm freaked out.'

'Hang on a sec – what's wrong with this thing?' Megan was fiddling with the satnav. 'Wait a minute – it's not configured. We're still eight miles away!'

It seemed that our confidence in the gadget had been misplaced. Megan hit a few buttons and there were some reassuring bleeping noises.

'OK – we're back on track!' the car swung round and we headed for the bright lights of the city.

Well, we were a bit late for the service but I don't think we missed much. It was fairly standard. A bit more liturgy than we were used to, but not bad. At one point the minister said ' . . . every single person in this room . . .', emphasizing the word single. He wasn't talking about dating at all, but we looked at each other and laughed because we knew exactly why we were there!

After the service they had real coffee and warm mince pies – very impressive. We had agreed on the way there that we would split up into ones, twos or threes in order to have a better chance of talking to some men. So that's what we did. Being brave and determined, I wandered off on my own and managed to get chatting to an associate pastor with an earnest way about him and piercing blue eyes. He was perhaps a little older than my upper age limit of 39, but I decided to make an exception. 'Looking good – looking promising,' I thought to myself. But then he took his hand out of his pocket and sure enough – there was the inevitable glint of gold on his wedding ring finger.

As I mentioned before, the glint of gold on the wedding ring finger of an interesting looking man is a very common sight. I am so used to seeing it nowadays that I get a shock when there is no flash of gold. The finger looks strangely naked and bald without it. It is a bit like the moment when Charlie finds the golden ticket in *Charlie and the Chocolate Factory* but in reverse, because when I see the gleam of gold my

That's the moment at which my heart skips a beat and hope springs up . . .

heart sinks. Then when there is no twinkle on the finger, but a twinkle in the eye, that's the moment at which my heart skips a beat and hope springs up . . .

Anyway, back to the story.

When we all reconvened outside the church, we discovered that this was wedding-ring central – every man seemed to be sporting a circle of gold, advertising his ineligibility. Nonetheless, we decided to head to the pub afterwards just in case. After chatting to a group of girls from the church for a while I discovered that there had been some frank and open discussion of singleness in the past at this church.

For example, there had been a series of talks about relationships. After one of these talks, all the single people were invited to the pub where there were a series of 'cringy' ice-breakers and then a debate, which turned into a slanging match across the room between girls and boys. Apparently the girls were yelling things like: 'Why can't you ask us out? Why is it such a big deal?'

To which the guys were replying: 'But if we do that you think we're asking you to marry us, when we certainly are not!'

At which the girls would counter with: 'We don't want instant marriage; we just want to know that the relationship isn't going to turn into another long-winded waste of time!'

. . . and so on.

The event sounds a bit uncomfortable and the resulting embarrassment must have lasted some time; but at least the church had recognized the existence of single people in their midst and was attempting to do something to get them together, even if it was a bit messy!

Discussion on the journey home revealed that Megan and Linda had done rather better than me on the bloke front. It appeared the elusive single men were hanging out up at their end of the table – just my luck! The men had even been bold enough to invite them to a Christmas party that was happening soon. So perhaps fishing in another pond can be successful? It sounds like a dating success to me!

Wedding belles and beaux

Encouraged by my friends' success at the new church, I stepped out with confidence into the next venture; which was to find myself a date amongst a wedding congregation. It was a good year to attempt this as I was going to no less than seven weddings – the first of which was in early April, the last in late September. Surely a date could be found at one of these lavish extravaganzas?

I do love weddings, and this season of festivities was no different. It was a smorgasbord of beautiful moments and colour, awash with love – from the exotic festooned jasmine of an Indian wedding to the delicate scent of lavender in an ancient barn in September. I am always delighted to see my friends and family taking that step of publicly declaring their devotion to one another. There really does seem to be nothing more romantic and hopeful than a couple making that lifelong promise to one another.

Anyway, I will not trouble you with all the details of those seven special days, but suffice to say that I did not find a single date amongst the whole lot. I think the reasons are manifold; but the chief ones are:

(1) You are invariably amongst friends at a wedding, and are thus less likely to meet someone new. However, if you have got hidden hopes of winning someone in your friendship group, a wedding could

be the ideal place to make your move. The atmosphere of heady romance will affect the object of your affection and may make them more receptive to your advances!

(2) At a wedding everyone is either a friend of, or related to, one member of the happy couple. So you are aware that if you try to ask someone on a date everyone will know about it, and will want to know the eventual result – including gruesome Auntie Susan, old Uncle Tom Cobley and all.

(3) You may have had a few afternoon drinks, and will thus be either hyper-aware of your own behaviour and therefore unwilling to talk to any strangers, or a little bit tipsy/drunken/sprawling/out-of-control/loud/self-pitying (circle as appropriate!) and off-putting to members of the opposite sex.

None of this is conducive to finding a date. So weddings seem to be less fertile hunting ground than I thought they might be.

Then there is the most important moment of the wedding day for all single women – the tossing of the bouquet. This tradition is met with a wide range of responses and produces curious behaviour at times. One of my friends went to a wedding where the females dutifully gathered round to catch, but when the bouquet was thrown they all avoided it, so there was a kind of 'reverse-scrum' effect, rather like a shoal of fish being parted by a predator, and the bouquet fell to the ground where it

Then there is the most important moment of the wedding day for all single women – the tossing of the bouquet

lay abandoned for some time until a non-plussed man picked it up. Then there was the wedding where a certain boyfriend tried to manoeuvre his girlfriend so that she caught the bouquet but she wasn't very keen to do so; or the wedding where men were doing the catching; or the one where an old maiden aunt of 88 caught the bouquet, much to the delight of everyone there. The last of these subsequently got married six months later. All these are myths and legends, and they may or may not be true.

What is true is that seven times that summer I took my place amongst the hopeful girls, and each time I felt absolutely sure that this time I would be the one to catch the bouquet. I have no idea where this bizarre confidence came from – I had not a scrap of evidence that it would happen, and yet I always believed it would. And sure enough, that summer my 'big moment' came.

It was at the wedding of two friends from church who were holding their ceremony in a Tree Cathedral. A Tree Cathedral is basically a forest that has been planted in the shape of a cathedral, so that you have the cross shape, the knave, the aisle and so on. It was all very beautiful and romantic: a spring wedding with bluebells, sunshine, a pink Cadillac, and a groom in a pork-pie hat. The invitation suggested wellingtons as suitable footwear, and I was very excited because I had actually managed to find a pair of wellies with wedge heels for the occasion. We had been having a great time, posing with friends and the Cadillac, tree-hugging (or hee-trugging as I mistakenly said!), and running through the sunny glade like a bunch of crazed pixies.

Anyway, when it was time for the bouquet, I had my usual firm feeling that this time I would catch it. I placed myself in the usual position – somewhere near the back, right in the middle of the bunch and, amazingly, this time it actually fell to me. Interestingly, the moment that the bouquet dropped into my hands was the moment that any hope of getting a date from this particular wedding disappeared. There was one guy I had been talking to and getting on with rather well, but as soon as I became 'bouquet girl', he vanished.

But it was so worth it.

I carried the gorgeous bouquet of purple irises, ferns, dried heather and white roses all the way home with me. My friend Sarah drove us back late at night through the dark forest and various villages. At one point some deer walked in front of the car, highlighted by the beam of our headlights – it was stunning. Then I caught a train, and attracted much interest and comment with my dress, wedding wellies, bouquet and bicycle. I must have explained a dozen times about the wedding and how I caught the bouquet. One friendly chap even said to me as he left the train, 'He's out there somewhere – bound to be, lovely girl like you – hope you find him soon!'

It was a very special feeling. The flowers felt like a blessing – like I was carrying my own trust and faith that one day it would work out and I would find someone to marry. The smile stayed for days. The flowers died, but I took lots of pictures of them, and I still have a small piece of the heather that I kept, which I think I will keep for ever to remind me of that day.

4

DATE OR MATE?

'Friendship often in love ends, but love in friendship never'
– ancient Chinese saying

I stepped off the train feeling that usual jolt of nervousness, and the familiar thought 'is this going to be bearable?' flashed up in my mind. Tony was standing near the ticket barrier, hands shoved deep in his pockets, trying not to look nervous. We gave each other the customary peck on either cheek.

Tony and I had met a few weeks earlier at a left-wing Christian conference all about saving the planet and campaigning for human rights. The conference turned out to be rather a good way of meeting potential dates. It was full of interesting, like-minded young Christian men (many of them rather too young and studenty perhaps but nonetheless . . .). There was even a delegates' book given out to each attendee, which had space for writing the names and contact details

One day I was feeling a little glum about how things were going (or not going)

of people you met – extremely useful for finding potential dates.

Tony and I had written our details on each other's booklet, and struck up an acquaintance on Facebook.

One day I was feeling a little glum about how things were going (or not going) with another man, and Tony must have read a self-indulgent Facebook status update because he got in contact with a cheery message suggesting that I come and explore his home town Leicester for the day. I thought why not – it would be another date notched up and it might be fun.

So there I was – stepping out into the sunshine of Leicester station with Tony that bright April day – and I felt great. It's funny how the nerves vanish as soon as you actually start talking to your date and you wonder whatever you were worrying about. He or she is just another person looking for love.

I felt really positive that morning. Tony seemed nice, Leicester was a new place to explore, the sun was shining. Spring was in the air . . .

However, I hadn't bargained on Charlotte.

As we walked to Tony's car a small blonde person in a bright pink coat and shiny pink shoes came running towards us with great energy and excitement. She was holding out her arms, chubby hands opened wide for a big hug.

'Tony! Tony!'

The small person leapt into Tony's arms.

'Oh! Hello, Charlotte!' he said, and he gave a growl as he picked her up – the kind a father might give.

The smile froze on my face. What was this? Did this small person actually belong to Tony? Was this small person coming on our date? I was completely confused, and resolved to just hold on tight and see what happened next.

At this point I became aware of a larger version of Charlotte coming up behind her.

'Hello. I'm Sarah.'

This was the only explanation I got before we all piled into the car. Tony and I were in the front; Charlotte and Sarah were in the back. As we drove through Leicester, Tony and I attempted conversation, but it was somewhat truncated:

'Well – this is Leicester then,' said Tony as he negotiated traffic.

'Great,' I began 'I've never actually . . .'

But I was never able to finish my sentence, because a small but imperious voice struck up from behind: 'Who's that, Mummy?'

'That's Becky,' replied Sarah patiently.

'Why?' . . . a slight pause . . .

Good question I thought – why am I Becky? We clearly had a philosopher in the car.

'Why what, sweet pea?'

'Why is she here?' said the small, imperious voice.

'She's Tony's friend.'

'Yes, Becky's my friend,' chipped in Tony indulgently, 'just like Amanat and Milly and Ben are your friends.'

'Why?' Charlotte clearly did not grasp the concept, or was choosing not to.

'Because she is,' said Mummy Sarah, slightly less patiently. 'Will you please stop wriggling, Charlotte?'

'I thought we might have some lunch then maybe go to the park,' tried Tony again.

'Is that lady coming to the park, Mummy?'

'Yes. Will you sit still please,' said Mummy Sarah in that angry-patient voice that only Mummies know how to use.

'Can I play on the swings?'

Sarah sighed.

And so the journey went on, with Tony and me barely able to exchange one word.

Bear in mind that I had only met Tony once before so this vanguard was more than a bit confusing. What kind of date was this? I felt like I had landed in the middle of a strange domesticity that I wasn't ready for at all. I sat in the passenger seat with a grin frozen onto my face thinking 'get me out of here!'

At long last, Charlotte went quiet – distracted by a bracelet that Sarah gave her, so Tony and I actually managed to get a bit of conversation going. I was as polite as possible, while trying to get to the bottom of what was actually going on here. It didn't make sense until Tony came out with the following:

'My girlfriend lives down in Dorset. She's doing a PhD.'

Ah! His girlfriend!

It was like all the lights went on at once.

This was not a date!

That's why Tony had brought Charlotte and Sarah – as a kind of protection, an indication that this was not a date. Suddenly it all made sense.

'We're here!

The four of us piled out and Tony led us to his home – a small hotel!

'You live in a hotel?!' I exclaimed.

'Yep.'

The hotel didn't have a single guest, and the family were away. It was like a ghost place – an old-world guest house with faded beauty. It smelt of mustiness and Crimplene.

The four of us piled out and Tony led us to his home – a small hotel!

We three adults went into the kitchen while Charlotte ran off. I leant against the counter and chatted to Sarah a bit. Tony had been rooting around in a cupboard and eventually emerged with a jar of sauce and a packet of slightly frozen chicken. He looked triumphant.

While Tony cooked, Charlotte and I played a honky-tonk out-of-tune old piano that we found in the study. Well, I say 'played' in the broadest sense. I attempted to sight-read some pieces from a children's song book, and Charlotte bashed the keys. It kind of worked.

After lunch Tony took me a on a guided tour of the place.

'The business is failing really badly. They're thinking of turning it into semi-permanent accommodation for church people. Charlotte and Sarah are going to live here too.'

I didn't ask where Charlotte's dad was, but I'd figured out by now that he wasn't Tony.

There was an old bar downstairs, with faded red leather chairs, empty brackets, and spirit measures with no spirit. Charlotte perched herself on one of the bar stools and was quickly mesmerised by some brightly coloured creatures prancing about on the giant TV screen.

The rest of us explored the guest rooms and the upstairs area where Tony lives with the family. The rooms were full of books, paint, toys – the detritus of a brood of children. I liked the fact that no-one had tidied things away. I liked that no-one had fixed the broken light in the bathroom – instead rigging up a temporary solution which involved trailing wires coming from the hallway and an angle-poise lamp planted in the middle of the bathroom floor. No-one had cleaned in a long time. Cats watched us with insouciant eyes. Outside the sun was still shining.

'Right – shall we go for that walk?'

Tony and I set out together, leaving the others behind. Charlotte had fallen asleep in the bar like a small barfly, drunk on children's television, and Sarah decided it was better to let her sleep. It was a bit of a relief to go out without them to be honest, even though Charlotte was a sweetie and Sarah was great. It's just that in order to meet an additional friend and her three-year-old daughter when on a date I do need to prepare myself mentally!

As we strolled through the park we chatted. I told Tony about the book and he was amused. Leicester was full of a mixture of friendly people. We ate ice cream, stood by a sparkling river and walked along the ruined walls of an old abbey. We talked about books, his girlfriend, space travel and protesting. In short, we had a lovely time and agreed to stay in touch at the end. But was it really a date?

The accidental date with the snow man

I have also had this situation happen in reverse, with me being the one who did not realize that I was in a dating situation. This is how it happened:

It was around the time of the snows of 2009. You know – the ones that we were totally unprepared for. We had been struggling with deep snow for almost a week, and I was on my way home from work. I happened to walk past a car that was stuck and decided to help push it out. Bad plan. I was pushing and heaving and straining, and the car was going nowhere. A man passing by saw this and decided to stop and help too. Of course, as soon as he put his shoulder to the car, it came free and went on its way. The rescue having been performed, we discovered that we were walking in the same direction, so we got chatting as we went. It turned out that he was a Christian as well, and seeing as I was fairly new to the area and wanted to make some friends I suggested we swap phone numbers.

So the snow man and I arranged to meet up the following weekend

So the snow man and I arranged to meet up the following weekend. His name, it turned out, was Nush. We had a lovely evening together where we got on very well, had a meal and went to see a film. I thought he was sweet and that I had a new friend, but he clearly had very different ideas. The next day, he texted, 'I don't think we should continue with this,' in a solemn and dramatic way, and I haven't seen or heard from him since. It just goes to show that two people can be on very different pages of the story book, and when this happens it is best to be philosophical and not get too upset about it.

How do you know if they want a date or a mate?

Of course, Tony didn't realize he was on a date at all, just as I didn't realize I was on a date with Nush. The way I met both these men did not lead to any firm indications of intentions. Tony's invitation was merely a friendly gesture from a pleasant guy, and I completely misinterpreted it as the action of a lovesick swain. My invitation to Nush was the same in reverse.

I did feel a little foolish, confidently strolling into the Tony situation, believing that he fancied me, when in fact he was just being friendly. And I felt sad that Nush was not able to simply be a friend.

So how do you avoid this situation? How do you know whether the new guy or girl you fancy or have befriended is meeting up with you because they want a partner, or because they want a friend?

The answer is – you have to ask them, because only they know. Swallow your pride and make your interest really, really obvious (without being creepy, weird or desperate). Just be upfront about it as soon as you can. If you like someone, be brave enough to tell them – it's the only way you will discover whether they feel the same – and also whether they have a boyfriend or girlfriend stashed away somewhere. Say that you'd really like to see them one-on-one sometime, to get to know them better. If you meet them within your friendship group, it could be trickier – but it is still a good idea to make your intentions clear as soon as possible. You will quickly discover whether or not they feel the same way.

Roll with it!

The other thing I learnt from these episodes is that when dating, you need to be prepared for anything and roll with the punches! You are going to have some mix-ups, some mistakes and misunderstandings. That's all part of the fun of finding your partner. And remember, none of it is serious until you've been on several dates together – so relax!

5

www.lookingforlove.com

'A bit forced.'
'People go on there with an agenda – they have a relationship in mind, not a person.'
'There are some real weirdoes on there – you never know who they really are.'
'Not for me.'

Above are some of the thoughts my friends shared when I told them I was making a foray into the complex and busy world of Internet dating. People often seem to see the Internet as a last resort when it comes to finding a partner – as though by the time you reach that stage you must be desperate. However, despite the reservations that many people have, dating via the Internet is becoming more and more common. I suspect that most of my single friends have tried Internet dating at some point, whether they would admit to it or not.

So, it was with some excitement and some tredipation that I began my cyber-journey

So, it was with some excitement and some

trepidation that I began my cyber-journey. As I searched, scanned and clicked I discovered that the world of online dating is a fascinating and complicated one. There is a vast array of sites available catering for every possible person. I quickly discovered that online dating is very labour intensive, and the job of replying to every message and sending out 'feelers' of your own is endless if you take it seriously! However, it is also a lot of fun. During my Internet research days I spent at least an hour online for two intensive weeks – searching, composing, replying and flirting.

The biggest challenge I found was actually the sign-up stage, when you have to present yourself and sell your positive qualities in the profile section. This is an initial hurdle that trips up many potential online daters right at the beginning, preventing them from even getting started. That's why I thought it might be useful to make this chapter a bit more 'hands on' than previous ones and give you some tips for filling out your profile so that you can try for yourself and get the most out of it that you can.

The profile

This is the all-important bit. It can seem quite daunting, as you have to answer dozens of questions about who you are, why you are, what you like, what you are for and who you want to find. Then you have to write a short essay about yourself, tick a zillion boxes, and upload photos . . . The process can feel so exhausting that by the time you are finished you no longer have any energy left to seek out potential dates. But don't worry – I've been through it all, and I'm here to help you get through the profile creation part of the process as quickly and efficiently as possible. Here is my short guide to creating an amazing profile that will make you shine like the star you are:

The photos!

Top tip: You must, must, must upload one! Even better, upload several.

This is so important, as you are far more likely to get people reading your profile if you feature a photo. It is the first thing that people will look at. So, which photos should you put up? Well, the main one should be your favourite recent photo of yourself – flattering, but true to life – showing your whole face – a 'mug shot'. The others can be a mixture, showing your life and the things you love – you with friends, on holiday in a special place, or taking part in a favourite activity. It is best to avoid photos of you in skimpy clothing, as it may attract the wrong sort of person. Also it is best to steer clear of compromising or drunken situations (not that you have any such photos I'm sure!).

The title

This needs to be short and sassy, and stand out from the crowd. It should grab attention and make people want to know more. It should also be unique to you and not state the obvious. So 'Positive happy girlie' is much less interesting than 'Olive-eating and rollercoaster-riding with a social conscience'. Try to think of your unique quirks and write them into that one sentence. It is a challenge, but quite fun. Ask a friend to help if you like.

The short essay

This is the bit where you get to tell the world who you really are and what you are looking for. As with the title, make it as unique as you can. Have fun with it, and don't resort to putting in things that everyone would put. At the same time, don't be kooky for the sake of being kooky – stick to being yourself. Obviously if you are eccentric then you can reflect this, but don't force it if you are not!

So if you spend your Saturdays sitting on the sofa in your pants watching football, say 'I enjoy sports'

Avoid saying things like 'I've never done this before' or 'I'm not the sort of person who usually does this kind of thing.' By saying this you would be suggesting that you are somehow 'above' Internet dating. If you think about it, you *are* doing it – so you might as well be proud of that fact and don't alienate the other people on the site before you have even started.

If you really are struggling to sell yourself, you could *get a friend to help you write your profile*. They are more likely to see you objectively and may well be more enthusiastic about your many excellent qualities than you would be yourself – they are your friend for a reason, remember. If your friend is single too you could return the favour and write their profile for them.

Don't lie on your profile

You are bound to get found out . . . unless you are planning to conduct your entire relationship in cyberspace until death do you part! Of course, having said this, you do want to put yourself in as positive a light as possible. So if you spend your Saturdays sitting on the sofa in your pants watching football, say 'I enjoy sports'. And if you have a tendency to be forgetful and dappy, put 'I am a dreamer, with a strong imagination'.

It's a bit like writing your CV. You are dressing yourself up in the best light possible, and everyone knows that you're going to accentuate the positive – so don't miss the opportunity to do it!

Make sure you fill in all the sections

If you don't bother, you just look lazy and risk coming across as someone who is not really taking the search seriously. Take a bit of time – do you want to find somebody or not?! Surely it's worth taking 20 minutes of your life to actually think about your profile carefully before writing anything. As a strategy, it is worth it because people will get the most rounded and true-to-life idea of who you actually are, and you are more likely to be spotted by the right person.

Other Top Tips

Be light-hearted and breezy

One important thing I learnt when starting online dating was to keep chirpy and to the point. Coming over all 'doom and gloom' doesn't get you very far in the world of dating. You wouldn't start a conversation with a stranger by telling somebody your entire life story, so why start an email exchange with a potential date that way? Just say hello – it's a perfectly acceptable start and it keeps you dignified and mysterious, rather than making you come across as a soggy bundle of emotion. Conversely, don't expect the person you are chatting with to tell you everything immediately. I remember talking to a friend who said she had gone on a dating site and started messaging a guy who looked quite interesting, but had been so disappointed by his one-line responses that she had given up. I think this is a shame. You can't expect someone to reveal all in an email – wait until you actually meet them for that! Which leads me on to:

Meet up 'in the flesh' as soon as you possibly can

You never really know how well you are going to hit it off until you actually meet, so try to sort out the face-to-face date as soon as you can . . . Remember that chatting online is a means to an end. You are doing this to meet somebody you actually like – not to flirt endlessly with online beings. Don't make the mistake of enjoying electronic chatting so much that you forget that your goal is to find someone real. Also, the longer you chat to somebody without meeting them, the higher the expectations. And the higher the expectations, the worse the nerves. And the worse the nerves, the greater the disappointment if he or she turns out to be not what they seemed onscreen. So get that first meeting arranged and out of the way as soon as you can. Then you will know quickly whether he or she is someone to follow up with.

And the higher the expectations, the worse the nerves – the worse the nerves, the greater the disappointment

To pay or not to pay?

There are lots of different ways of doing the Internet dating thing. Some sites provide an entirely free service. Others have various options for membership that can give you certain advantages over other people on the site; or which will find you tailored dates based on shared interests or backgrounds.

If you think of your search for a partner as an investment for the future, and focus on what could come out of it, you may well decide to choose one of the paying options. The advantages include matching services, profile visibility and contact details. The other thing to consider is that people who pay for their online dating are likely to be a lot more serious about finding a partner than those who are casually dipping a toe into the world of cyber-matchmaking. So if you opt to pay, you increase your chances of finding someone worthwhile.

I chose to go for the free options because of my limited time and the scope of my research. Even with the minimum profile, I was still able to find three men willing to meet me within the space of two weeks. I think this was partly due to the time and effort I put into writing my profile, the fact that I put plenty of pictures up, and the fact that I was on there every day developing my contacts. However, if I had more time I would have paid for one of the matching services that some websites provide, for example the matching service from Network Christians (see below).

If you do decide to pay for your Internet search, make sure that you have investigated all the websites that are out there and have found the option that is best for you before paying up. There are so many to choose from, you want to be sure that you are going for the right one, and that doesn't necessarily mean the cheapest deal. Surely it has to be worth paying a little more for a quality service that will find you people who you can really connect with.

And for my final tip . . . *please don't write poetry.*

One day I logged in to my profile on UK Dating, and saw a little yellow smiley face with a wink sitting in my inbox. I hopefully double-clicked and was met with the following:

Roses are red,
Violets are blue,
You are beautiful
Will I do?

I had absolutely no idea how to respond to this. Unfortunately the man in question was 52, so it wasn't going to go anywhere. But even if he had been 32 I would have been a bit non-plussed. It is better (in my opinion) to try saying hello first or asking about a person's day or their interests, and save the odes and sonnets for a later date . . .

The horror!?

Everyone has heard some horror stories about Internet dating. One of my friends met a man on BigChurch – a Christian dating site – who had a rather unusual interest. He was into large-breasted ladies – not unusual. He also liked an older lady – fair enough. However, when they met, it turned out that his fascination with breasts went beyond the usual. They met up several times, and were getting quite cuddly on the sofa one evening. That was when he shared his breast feeding fantasy with my friend. Well she ran a mile, as you can imagine.

Another male friend of mine went on a date with a woman who had an argument with him over the phone before they had even met. She was apparently livid because he had arranged to meet her at the station rather than picking her up in his car. As you can probably imagine, the date itself did not go well.

Then there was the friend who took a girl he met to a sushi bar, but she turned out to be allergic to shellfish

Then there was the friend who took a girl he met to a sushi bar, but she turned out to be allergic to shellfish – he ended up spending the night in A & E.

Another friend met somebody whose profile said she was 22 and she turned out to be 42. Her profile was a complete fabrication.

However, my experience of Internet dating was really not as alarming or exciting as any of this. I met up with three men from the Internet and they were all very ordinary, decent guys just trying to find someone to love. There was Tomas – a biochemist from Hungary with a bad temper; Italian Eduardo who took me to the theatre and wanted emotion and devotion that I couldn't give; and John – who was sweet but never made a move. They were all very ordinary and nice.

I was probably a little more nervous than usual when meeting up with them all for the first time because of how we met. But other than that, these dates were no different to any of the other dates I went on.

If you are very reluctant to search for love online I would urge you to give it a try. The more people you meet the more chance you have of meeting 'the one', so how can it possibly be a bad thing? Also, I know for a fact that Internet dating can and does work. How do I know? My American cousin married her musician boyfriend earlier this year. They met on Match.com. Let that encourage you as you get clicking your mouse!

Some websites for you to try:

Christian sites

www.networkchristians.com – *free online dating service, paid matching service*

I really like this one so I have put it first. It is a very real Christian site run by people who genuinely care about single people in the church. The people I met on the site were down to earth, friendly and varied. Network Christians also do excellent days out to places in the UK. I went on one to Oxford and met some lovely people, including staff from the organization. The range of ages was good – from mid-twenties up to forties and fifties. There was a friendly atmosphere, and the organizers were quite upfront about their spirit-led desire to help single Christians in their search for a life partner.

Network Christians also do a paid-for personal introductions service, where they interview you extensively and then match you up with suitable partners on their database. This costs £60 for a year. I didn't try it because I didn't have enough time, but I think it is excellent value and money very well spent – a good investment in finding your partner. I know several established couples from my work and church who met via this particular agency. The only downside for me was that there were fewer men than women on the website when I was using it. Other than that, Network Christians comes highly recommended for all age groups.

www.bigchurch.com – *free with 'pay for' features*

This one is quite easy to use and navigate. However, there are a lot of people on it outside the UK which could be difficult in terms of meeting up with each other (though I do know couples who have struck up inter-continental relationships via websites that have led to marriage). The people who run it also run several other 'special interest' dating sites, some of which are a little bit . . . unusual . . . so the Christian angle may not be entirely genuine.

www.christianmingle.com – *free with 'pay for' features*

This one is a bit complicated to use. It also claims to be free, but quickly asks for money once you are on the site having completed all the questions.

www.christiancafe.com

This site is good. You get a free ten-day trial, but after that you have to pay.

Secular sites

www.parship.co.uk **www.eharmony.co.uk** – *both have free features, but you will have to pay for the bits that work the best*

These sites use personality profiling to find people who match you. It takes a lot of the effort out of doing the searches yourself, and can get some good results. They are not specifically Christian, but will pull up other Christians for you if you specify that's who you are looking for. Be warned – there are a *lot* of questions to answer, so give yourself a good hour and a half set-up time.

www.match.com – *you get a free trial, but then they trick you by not allowing you to see any photos!*

One of the best-known and most effective dating sites there is. This is where my cousin met her husband. This really was the most comprehensive and user-friendly site I looked at. Match.com is definitely worth the money, and it matches personalities very well. As a member, I went on a lovely date to the Natural History Museum with a man called Graham. The only downside is that the number of committed Christians on there is small.

This list is not exhaustive and there are many more options out there . . . Have fun in your search!

Searching the Book of Faces

Of course there is also **www.facebook.com** – you might have heard of it?! I spent a few happy hours looking for interesting Christian men who my friends were 'friends' with. The search yielded some interesting finds, but no-one that I actually had the courage to contact out of the blue. Apart from anything else it felt wrong – a bit like stalking, and I was worried about the potential repercussions for my friends. In fact I am quite embarrassed to admit to my Facebook investigations here, but I am relying on the fact that most of us have done it at some time. Please tell me I am not alone?!

I did have one small success on Facebook, managing to ask out one guy who I had met in 'real-life' at a wedding. I looked him up, befriended him, then asked whether he might like to meet up some time in as casual a way as I could. It turned out he had a girlfriend (who he had neglected to say anything about on his Facebook profile), but he seemed flattered to be asked. I was glad that I had tried, and not too embarrassed. So everyone was happy. A quite straightforward and non-creepy way to ask someone out, though I do think it helped that I had actually met him in the flesh – otherwise it would have been odd.

So Facebook as a follow-up tool, yes; but Facebook as a primary method of contacting strangers – definitely not.

6

SPEED DATING

'A loving heart is the beginning of all knowledge'
– Thomas Carlyle

Going speed dating is one thing, going speed dating towards the end of a week-long Christian festival is quite another. Imagine the scenario. You have been camping for five days. The rain has been pouring down. You forgot your wellies so your flip-flop clad feet are entering a stage of filthiness you hitherto only suspected could exist (in fact, you are slightly worried that you are going down with trench foot or one of those other foot problems that soldiers got in the First World War, when they had to march for miles through mud). Your hair is in shock. You are without make-up, perfume or flattering clothes. You suspect that you are beginning to smell like a pond that needs cleaning due to the fact that you have been rain-drenched for the last week. And you are going on not one, but several short dates where you want to create the best impression you possibly can.

This is the situation I found myself in at New Wine in July 2009.

I was working there and two festival friends from the café suggested we go together. Well, I was very glad of

Our compère for the evening was a fearsome lady – forceful yet strangely negative

the company at the beginning. We sat together, sipping our cheap wine from plastic glasses. One of the girls, Esther, had somehow acquired some perfume and we were passing it round. As I sprayed liberally I wondered whether it was going to cover up the pervasive smell of mud that was hanging around me.

Curiously, all the women had gathered at one end of the room and all the men at the other. I suppose this is not altogether surprising, seeing as we were about to embark on one of the most potentially embarrassing exercises in the world of dating – the speed date.

We were each armed with a number badge, a piece of paper with everyone else's number on it and a pencil. The idea was that as we went round, we would tick 'yes', 'no' or 'friend' for each person that we chatted to.

Our compère for the evening was a fearsome lady – forceful yet strangely negative – a totally unsuitable combination for speed dating, which should definitely be done with a light touch. This lady was pressuring us all from the front – practically heckling us to interact. But then she came out with: 'If you can't find anyone you want to talk to, you can have your money back.'

This declaration startled me out of a perfectly OK conversation that I was having with a quite pleasant man. I hadn't had any complaints up to that point, and was taken aback. When I looked around, though, I realized what the problem was. A clutch of displeased-looking women was standing to one side, refusing to talk to anyone. I thought that this was strange and a bit rude of them, but as I looked around again I realized that most of the men in the room were very much younger than the women – by at least ten years.

I shrugged my shoulders and got stuck back in.

The second guy I spoke to was very interesting – a student of philosophy, intelligent, articulate, good looking . . . and 19 years old! Nearly ten years younger than me!

We moved on. I ticked 'friend'.

The third guy I spoke to grinned and said, 'My vicar would kill me if he knew I was doing this.'

Why? How utterly absurd. It's not as if we were fornicating there in the tent. I suppose that it could be argued that speed dating commodifies the search for a partner, but from my point of view, all I was doing was having a small glass of wine and chatting to a few members of the opposite gender. How on earth could anyone condemn this activity, which might actually result in some people getting together, getting married and some long-term happiness?! I articulated this viewpoint to him in a pretty forthright manner (helped along by the wine perhaps). He seemed to appreciate my point, but then moved right into my personal space and started to smirk and sleaze. I actually had to back away from him. This man definitely seemed to have got the wrong idea as to what speed dating was about, and he had taken my comments as some kind of green light to be really odd.

We moved on – thankfully. I ticked 'no'.

The fourth guy had the smallest and most ridiculous beard I have ever seen in my life. It looked like someone had dipped their little finger in ink and dabbed it on his chin, just under the lower lip – a tiny fingerprint of hair – 'boop' – just like that! I found the beard so distracting. I couldn't take my eyes off it, and couldn't form any thought apart from 'beard'! He was talking about something; I have no idea what – my eyes were on the tiny beard for five whole minutes, watching it jump up and down as he spoke.

We moved on. I ticked 'friend' and wrote 'beard' for my own reference.

The next guy was really nice. We had a good chat about music, our churches, God. We were enjoying it so much that we actually kept chatting for half an hour instead of moving on, but eventually we had to part.

And so it continued . . . the peculiar dance of strangers in search of love.

At the end of the evening all of our papers were collected and we went back to our tents. The results would be out the next morning . . .

The sweet moment

So I suppose you want to know – did I get any matches?

Well, because this was a festival speed date, instead of being emailed our results we had to go to the information tent to collect them the following day at 1 p.m. So there we were, lined up expectantly. It felt a bit like getting the results of A-levels, or a medical examination. The Information Lady at the desk also had the air of a school teacher about her, with spectacles and pulled-back hair.

I was genuinely nervous as I stood in line, not least because the one guy I had liked the most was standing right in front of me

I was genuinely nervous as I stood in line, not least because the one guy I had liked the most (the one who I chatted with for half an hour, both of us sneakily refusing to move on) was standing right in front of me – wearing a hat for disguise perhaps, but unmistakably him!

I decided I couldn't be bothered with being shy.

'Hello.'

'Oh, hi.'

Awkward smiles exchanged.

'Want a sweet?' I offered him one from the bowl on Information Lady's desk.

'Sure,' he said, and I handed him one.

There was a pause.

'Well, this is weird,' I said through a mouthful of toffee.

And it was truly weird.

He took his hat off and wiped his brow in a semi-mocking way with an edge of seriousness.

'Phew, I can't take this – we are about to be judged. "Nobody likes you – you are Officially Unlovable. Go home now."'

I laughed, but before we could continue it was my turn to go forward and get my results.

I stepped forward and gave my name.

The Information Lady riffled through the small white envelopes piled on her desk. I watched as her fingers turned each one carefully over. Her forehead above the spectacles grew more and more wrinkled as the pile got smaller and smaller. The pile dwindled and then was finished. The Information Lady took off her spectacles and looked directly at me with a sympathetic shrug.

'I'm sorry, dear, there's nothing here for you.' My heart sank, but then she continued: 'It means you have a match, but there's something wrong with our computers so you'll have to come back later today or tomorrow to pick up your results.'

At that moment she seemed like an angel sent from heaven. Or at least the most sympathetic Information

Lady I had ever encountered. She seemed to genuinely care. I'm sure I saw her wink as I turned to go.

I walked out, giving a brief smile to the man in the hat as I went. He smiled back. Feeling slightly weird and light-headed I decided to walk very slowly . . . A moment later he caught up with me.

'So . . .?' I asked.

'Well, I've got a match, but I don't know who.'

'Me too.'

'Weird.'

'Yeah,' he said. 'Weird.'

We paused awkwardly for a moment, not quite sure what to do.

'Well, I've got to go – bye then,' I said.

'Um . . . OK, bye.'

We headed in different directions – confounded and befuddled in my case!

So, we both returned to the information tent later in the day (separately this time thank goodness). The Information Lady handed me my envelope with a special sort of speed-dating results smile.

'You have a lovely day, dear.'

I walked away from the desk, feeling a combination of ridiculously excited and nervous, and once I was outside the office I ripped open the envelope.

When you read the words 'Congratulations – you have a match' and you like the person, it is a bit like Christmas morning when you are a kid. A lovely, happy, yummy feeling in your stomach – someone cool likes you and you have the proof in your hand!

Where you go from there is up to you, your match and God I guess.

And if you don't have any matches, well – you haven't lost anything, and you got a night out. So try again and again!

Never, ever give up

At this point I would like to draw attention to the power of persistence. The week before I went on this speed date I stood in the sitting room doorway of my house and gave my flatmate Atheist Andy earache about how I might as well give up and decide to be a spinster for ever more; about how I was a hopeless case who seemed to make everything go wrong and how none of it was worth it anyway. It was a very dark moment, which I'm sure we all get from time to time. Then four days later everything changed – I went on the speed date and had a very promising date lined up.

I might as well give up and decide to be a spinster for ever more

Sometimes, quitting is the saddest thing to do. At the same festival where I went speed dating, I met a lovely 40-year-old lady called Rachel who told me that she went through exactly this thought process fifteen years earlier at the age of 25 and came to the decision to 'shelve the whole relationship thing' (as she put it).

We got chatting one day over lunch and I told her about the speed date which was to take place that evening. I asked whether she was going. She said no – she wouldn't have the courage for something like that, and laughed a little. I tried every method of persuasion to get her to come, but she wouldn't. She was very interested in the idea though, and she said one particular thing that stuck in my mind: 'I suppose it might be even more special if two people who were just right for each other were to meet later in life.'

That's when she told me that she had wanted to find someone when she was 25, but decided the best thing to do was to put that side of herself away, to fold it up like an old summer dress, put it on a top shelf, and never look at it again. She felt that God had better things in store.

Rachel was lovely. We kept bumping into each other over the course of the festival, and even had the chance to pray for each other. She was small, mouse-like and somehow ageless. She spoke in a whisper, as soft as autumn leaves falling from the trees. She had long grey hair, big luminous blue eyes and a shy smile. She shone with a special light that was unique to her.

She is still out there somewhere, this lady. And I'm sure she could yet find someone, she is so charming. But I don't know whether she will ever have the courage to look . . . or even whether she can believe that God might have plans for her in that respect. It makes me sad.

That's why I'm determined to keep hoping. I truly believe that God doesn't want anyone to be lonely, or sad, or squished by life. If he has put the desire for a life partner in your heart, he has put it there for a reason – and you do have permission to pursue that dream. If he's telling you clearly that you are going to be with someone, you have to keep cheerfully trusting him and acting to find that person at the same time. God being God, he will sometimes bring you to a very low point before the ascent can begin. But please don't lose hope in the low places – keep believing and keep looking!

Taking no prisoners

So back to speed dating: a form of searching that takes no prisoners and leaves no room for doubt. There is no room for 'just getting to know someone and seeing where it goes'. You have a set time of five minutes with the other person – eight minutes if you are lucky – and you have to decide within that tiny window of opportunity, whether or not you would like to see this person again for a full date.

The advantages of speed dating are that it cuts out all the messing around and the umm-ing and ahh-ing

The advantages of speed dating are that it cuts out all the messing around and the umm-ing and ahh-ing that so often goes along with friendship between the sexes – all the misread signals and hurt feelings. Speed dating is as simple as putting a tick in the box – or so its proponents would say.

Speed dating takes many different forms, and if you are at all nervous about this sort of venture, I would advise that you check out what type of speed dating experience you are going to be part of before you pay out your money and get dolled up ready to go.

Here are a few of the more common types:

- The formal speed date. This is carried out through tête-à-têtes across small tables decorated with a single candle. A bell tinkles and the man moves on, the music and lighting are low, the patrons serious and intent on finding their mate, the conversations invariably dull and indistinguishable from one another. Everything is done strictly to time and copious notes are taken.
- The informal speed date. This is quite chaotic, as it involves groups of people circulating and chatting at

random. It is less controlled, but leaves more opportunity for talking to someone at length if you hit it off (because no-one notices if you don't move on).

- The double speed date. In this form, pairs of men move from table to table chatting to pairs of women. This takes some of the awkwardness out of the experience, and makes it more light-hearted. You can go with a friend and know that they will be there as your wing-man (or woman). I found the conversations to be more fun and the atmosphere lighter.
- The fundraising speed date. Speed dating has become popular as a way of raising money for your favourite charity. The problem with this is that you tend to know everybody who is there. You have fun, but end up with all your ticks in the friend box.
- The more exotic forms of speed dating involve locks and keys, and curious games. This type of event did not come within my remit when researching this book as I could not find a group of Christians willing to give this a go!

As mentioned above, I would strongly recommend doing your research before you go to a speed-dating event. What follows is a true-life example of an occasion where I failed to read the small print . . .

The wrong speed-dating session

'You here for Stepping Stones?' asked the man on the door, gruffly. 'You're early.'

Marion and I meekly apologized and paid our five pounds each. I picked up a yellow A4 sheet of paper from a stack on the welcome desk: *'Stepping Stones news, Dec '08. Helping unattached over 40s enjoy the Single Life!'*

'Unattached over-40s'. Ah. I was in my late 20s. Marion was a little older (I won't say by how much).

I must admit my heart had sunk a bit when I read the 'over-40s' part

This was going to be interesting.

We shuffled in. There were plenty of seats to choose from, so we chose the most innocuous looking table and sat facing out into the room so as to look more welcoming. Admittedly there was nobody to look welcoming towards at that moment, but we were determined that when the time came we would be ready to welcome!

I must admit my heart had sunk a bit when I read the 'over 40s' part. But on discussion with Marion, I decided it wasn't so bad. My upper age limit is ten years older; but I guess I could stretch to 42 or 43 . . . In fact the older man has a certain charm – experience, stability, wisdom . . . Maybe this wouldn't be so bad.

After about five minutes a Person walked in. This Person was dressed in a pale brown fake fur coat, expensive looking jewellery and lots of make-up. She had a wonderful deportment, seeming to float across the room and into a chair at the table next to ours. Once seated, she sipped her drink and demurely contemplated us, her neighbours. We introduced ourselves and the Person introduced herself as Margaret. She was other-worldy. Must have been 60 but looked like a well-preserved film star.

The next people to enter were two slightly scruffy, earthy, normal looking women – a bit of a relief after Margaret. They bought drinks and plonked themselves down at our table, saying that we looked welcoming (it worked!). Then another group arrived – three more women. Hmm . . . This was starting to get concerning. Where were the men?

'Perhaps there won't be any men,' I whispered to Marion.

Marion looked philosophical. 'Well, we can still have a good time if so. After all, it is a social group, not a dating agency.'

I looked sceptical.

But then . . . joy of joys. A man walked in. OK, he looked at least 65, but at least he was male.

Then another one walked in. This one was more promising. He actually had dark hair rather than grey. And he had a long dark coat that made him look like a detective. I could feel the various women in the room observing him, and I did the same myself.

He stood at the bar looking nervous and bought a beer. After downing the beer he put the glass down decisively and strode out of the door.

'He's gone,' I said to Marion and the other ladies on our table.

'Who's gone?'

'The man. The one in the dark coat.'

'Perhaps he's gone to the toilet.'

'No – that's definitely the exit.'

'He's escaped!'

'Oh no – they can't escape. That's why they put bouncers on the door.'

Peals of laughter.

'Perhaps he's gone to put his coat in the car.'

And sure enough he had. After a moment he was back, standing at the bar again – this time without a coat.

'Hmm . . . I preferred him with the coat,' mused one of the ladies.

I thought she was being a bit mean, but if I was honest I could see what she meant. Without his coat the man looked kind of deflated, like a punch-bag that has taken one too many hits.

So the place filled up nicely, and it was time for the 'Speed Mixing'. This is like speed dating, except that you move round in pairs so that you are talking in a group of four rather than one-to-one.

I must admit I was a little nervous as we were taken to meet our first pair; but actually I was pleasantly surprised by the whole thing. The men were all extremely polite and gentlemanly. There was no swearing, no excessive drunkenness, no leering. I was more than happy to talk to all of them, and there were some great characters.

A few people really stand out in my memory.

There was a 70-year-old carpenter who claimed to have built most of Milton Keynes. He moved here before it even existed. He was sprightly and slim and the first on the dance floor which was a joy to see.

There was a comedy duo comprising a large, loud bailiff and a tiny mole-like man. The bailiff had a roaring laugh that sounded like four men laughing from one throat. He laughed a lot. The small one said he enjoyed hang-gliding and was a part-time Eskimo (at least it sounded like 'Eskimo', it was very hard to hear anything over the bailiff's roaring laugh).

There was a guy from Liverpool who looked just like Ringo Starr and whose cousin plays drums for the band 'Muse'.

There was an opera fan whose granddaughter – another Becky – does ballet.

And there was Tim – the man in the coat. He was a history teacher and had been for eighteen years. (That explained the punch-bag look.)

History – now that's something there was a lot of that night. Almost every man I spoke to had been married before. Many had children as well. The most common questions I was asked were 'So, Becky, have you been married?' and 'How many children have you got?' (It wasn't a Christian event by the way, in case you hadn't worked that out!)

For some of them, Stepping Stones was a way of life. They'd been coming to the social club so long they had actually forgotten why they were there. But at least they were having a good time. The memory of that carpenter grooving on the dance floor will stay with me a long time.

Good for him!

Top tips for speed dating:

- ♥ Check the age-range of the event before you go. I have never been so popular in my life as I was at the over-40s event, but it didn't produce any serious possibilities!
- ♥ If you chat to someone and you are not sure if you like them, tick yes – they might grow on you after a date!
- ♥ Don't get drunk (not that you would, good Christian folk that you are).
- ♥ For goodness sake don't take it seriously or have any expectations!

My speed date man didn't work out in the end, though we did meet up a few times. If you follow the advice above you will have a good time, you won't disgrace yourself and you may even find someone you rather like.

7

JAW JAW

'Conversation about the weather is the last refuge of the unimaginative'
– Oscar Wilde

Conversation is one of the greatest pleasures we have in life. A good talk can do wonders. When I am assessing a potential new soul mate, I often ask myself: 'Has he got *The Talk*?'

The Talk is a very special thing, and a very essential thing. It is not 'being talkative'; rather it is talking just enough, about just the right things, with just the right number of funny jokes. It is hard to define and I have no doubt it differs from person to person. *The Talk* is more than topics, it is a feeling and a style that sets you at ease and makes you interested. When *The Talk* is there you are comfortable and things seem to fit.

However, if you end up on a date with someone who clearly doesn't have *The Talk*, do not despair – you can still have a good time and you may learn something. To illustrate this point, here's a story about a date I went on where *The Talk* was not present, and yet I had a good time and learnt something new . . .

The granny, the gorillas and the man who didn't go to war

I met James in the pub after church one day. I was sitting there with my friends and they asked the inevitable question: how was the search for dates going? I told them the latest news – the dates I'd been on – disasters and successes. A new guy was sitting with the group; a handsome bald-headed guy who seemed to be quietly weighing everyone up. After making inquiries he found out about the book and his face lit up.

Yes – sure – I'll be a date. I want to be famous!

'I'll be a date!'

'Really?'

'Yes – sure – I'll be a date. I want to be famous!' he practically bounced up and down in his chair with excitement at the thought.

I felt slightly awkward, taken aback by his enthusiasm. 'I usually change the names.'

'Well, you don't need to with me . . .' then his face suddenly closed up '. . . unless you say something mean.'

'Well I can't guarantee that,' I said, 'but I can give you the option to read-through before I publish.'

'Agreed,' he said. We shook on it and he laughed with his whole mouth – a head-thrown-back mouth-roaring laugh. When he laughed he made gorilla noises and slapped his thighs. This was slightly disturbing, but it did give me the idea for where we could go on our date.

I left the pub a happy girl. I had found my next date!

Going to the zoo!

As the date day approached I was very excited, and rightly so. We were going to the zoo! James and I had been exchanging overexcited text messages about it, the best from him was:

'I'm a little worried they might lock me up as part of the attractions!'

So, after church on a sunny spring day, we set out in his car for London. At first the atmosphere was light and happy – the open road, the prospect of animals to stare at, the nostalgia of going back to a beloved place from childhood.

But as time went on, it began to seem like the day was doomed. First of all we got lost. Then the traffic got steadily heavier and heavier until we were hardly moving. Sometimes you can make light of this and enjoy the dilemma, but in this case it wasn't going to happen. James was getting quite angry – I could feel the bristling tension coming off him and I didn't really know how to respond to it. The date that I was looking forward to the most was turning out to be a disaster.

By this time our car had come to a complete standstill. We were listening to Michael Jackson to try and cheer ourselves up, but it wasn't working and just seemed to be heightening the tension. James prodded a button and the music disappeared. I stared out into the hot London street. Shops with vegetables piled outside: some familiar, some exotic; all the multi-coloured people of London going about their Sunday business. Then, out of the melee, a little old lady appeared. She was attempting to cross the road in front of us, ever so painfully and slowly. We watched for a moment as she tottered and swayed, her stick wobbling dangerously. That was when James muttered something inaudible under his breath, opened the car door and went up to help her.

I was slightly nervous about being left in a stationary car in the middle of the road. But it was kind of sweet really – the blokey, bald-headed guy offering the little old lady his arm; a picture of chivalry.

Unfortunately the little old lady didn't seem to want to take the proffered arm – not in the least. In fact, she seemed to think that she was being assaulted and responded accordingly – battering him with her handbag and screeching. James shielded his head with his arms and retreated rapidly back to the car. The little old lady, who had developed a hitherto unseen turn of speed, pursued him waving her stick. James jumped in, slam-med the door, and we made our getaway. The traffic had mysteriously cleared and James' car took us away from the scene of the crime faster than the best pair of criminals London has ever seen. We left the little old lady waving her fist, still firmly implanted in the middle of the road.

So we purchased two large hot dogs with the works and perched on rickety white plastic chairs to eat them

'Well, that was interesting,' I proffered.

James grunted.

Food faux-pas

When we finally arrived at the zoo, it was only a couple of hours from closing time.

Pushing our way through the families, buggies and screaming children James said, 'I'm starving.' We purchased two large hot dogs with the works and perched on rickety white plastic chairs to eat them, trying to ignore the rubbish and squished mess left on the table by the last family.

As we ate James kept looking at me strangely. I couldn't figure out why until he said, 'Er – you've got mustard on your nose.'

'Oh – where?' I dabbed at my nose randomly.

'Not quite.'

'There?'

'Left a bit.'

'Yes? Gone?'

'Nearly.'

'Gone now?'

'Yep.'

I was left sitting there feeling sure the mustard hadn't quite gone and intermittently rubbing the offending spot whilst simultaneously trying to eat the rest of my hot dog without further misadventure.

'Want an ice cream?' asked James when I had completed the long process of finishing my hot dog in an elegant way.

'Sure – you choose me one.'

So he did. For himself he bought a 99 flake. For me he chose a long stripy one, which was quite possibly the worst shape of ice cream ever invented. Suffice to say, it was more difficult to eat in a flattering way than the hot dog. I decided the best approach was to attack from the bottom and it promptly fell off the stick.

Gorilla kingdom

I was glad when we had finished our meal and could go and find some animals to look at.

'Where first then?' I asked him

The reply came without hesitation: 'Gorillas!'

We entered 'Gorilla Kingdom' through a big green plastic flap. There was a lot of build up and added drama before we reached the big grumpy apes themselves. As it turned out, these gorillas were no fun at all. They seemed thoroughly depressed, sitting with their backs to us – I could feel their animosity. James enjoyed seeing them, but I was not impressed.

We headed onwards, through the butterfly house – warm, damp and full of mystery – with chrysalises hanging like jewels and atlas moths flapping past. Then into the snake house – picking out the shapes of the long, lethal creatures. Then through the giraffe pen – with the tall pink doors – the residents visibly drooping with the burden of their confinement.

Next we walked through monkey land. Why do monkeys always do rude things in the zoo – poo-flinging, scratching, farting? My theory is that they are thoroughly fed up with people staring at them. The ones we saw on that day mostly showed us their bums and tried to wee on us.

Then into the aquarium where slick fish darted through dirty tanks. And the aviary where humming birds buzzed like fat, shiny insects. And the jackal pen where the hungry dogs ran together, following each visitor.

At the end of the day, the tiger paced her cage, waiting for food. We caught our breath and watched, entranced as she leapt from platform to platform, moving quickly along the inside of the fence. Her breath came in soft growling pants that coincided with each footstep. For the first time that day, I felt the power of the wild.

Then the tiger pointed her bum at the gathered audience.

'She'd better not squirt,' said James under his breath, then louder as though he was in some kind of submarine action movie: 'SHE'S GONNA BLOW!'

'She'd better not squirt,' said James under his breath, then louder as though he was in some kind of submarine action movie

People looked round at James shouting. At the exact same moment a spray of musky liquid came out of the tiger's bum, drenching a small child's hair and sending him bawling.

As we walked away I looked at James wryly: 'You know, I think you might have prophetic gifts.'

He grinned. 'I just think like an animal, that's all.'

'Ladies and gentlemen, the zoo is now closing – will you please make your way to the exits.'

Home time already. It felt like we had only just arrived.

'Let's go and say goodbye to the gorillas,' James suggested with a glint in his eye.

'I don't know. I think it's closed.'

'Come on!'

So we ducked under the fence, through the green flap, and there they were. This time it was just us and them. James leant towards the moat, draping his arms across the fence.

One of the males ran across, pummelling his chest with that hollow-barrel sound.

'Wow!' James pummelled his chest in imitation. 'Awesome!'

The gorilla stared back with suspicion. His gaze moved to me. I shrugged my shoulders and pulled an apologetic face, at which the gorilla turned his back and we decided it was time to leave.

The soldier who didn't go to war

Later, James and I were driving home, and the subject turned to his previous vocation as a marine. This does not sit very well with me, and I was starting to get animated about the theme:

'I don't agree with war. You can't be a Christian and be a war-like person. Jesus said to turn the other cheek.'

'You're a pacifist?!' he looked at me incredulously and laughed.

'I suppose so, yes – inasmuch as I can't see that there is ever such a thing as a good war.'

'A good war?' he snorted. 'War isn't good or bad. It just is. That's all.'

'But you can't say that – 'it just is' – your opinion counts you know.' I was getting really worked up now. 'Imagine if everyone in the Army just decided to say, "No thanks – I don't like war – this isn't for me." We would have peace on earth instantly.'

'You're sounding like John Lennon now.'

'I'd rather be a pacifist than a pawn in someone else's war game.'

There was a small silence.

'Did you ever go to war?' I asked.

'No.' James was silent; then he began again. 'I'm so glad that I got out when I did; that I never got sent to Iraq. Every person I know who went out has come back completely crazy. Even ordinary people who had no problems at all before. It's the craziness of having to follow orders without questions. But you don't want to hear about this – it's a bit of a downer.'

'I do want to hear.'

'Well, the madness of it is that you can be chatting away to an Iraqi family – getting to know them, giving the kids sweets and pencils and stuff. You can be laughing and joking with a local soldier. But then as soon as the order comes from above, you've got to go and kill that solider who has become your friend. You've got to drop a bomb on that family with the sweet kids. It's really messed up.'

Yeah – people get hate mail, poo posted through their doors . . .

'Well, I guess that's what I was trying to say when I said all war is bad.'

'But you know, what really makes me sick is when the soldiers come back from Afghanistan or Iraq and these middle class idiots who don't know anything about anything start giving them abuse for being out there.'

'Really?'

'Yeah – people get hate mail, poo posted through their doors . . . And they are already suffering enough with the guilt of what they've been involved in. What these interfering people don't realize is that the soldiers don't have any choice. They are literally just following orders. And it can screw them up so badly having to kill like that. It's not their fault.'

I felt really humbled by this conversation. I had seen something from the inside that I had always had strong opinions about but had never really understood.

We went to church after this to catch the evening service. It was a relief to be in the presence of God but also surreal. We entered the service at the end, at the ministry stage. Some people were crying, some were laughing or shaking while soft guitar music played. I looked at the young people in there and wondered what struggles they were bringing to God that evening. I thought about the petty difficulties I sometimes bring before God – especially my own little problems with men.

I thought about the family in Iraq. The children running in the dust and laughing. Their mothers keeping them in check. The amicable soldiers on either side who had nothing against each other but had become pawns in a game of power that is so big and terrible they are powerless against it. And I felt ashamed and small. I looked at James and realized I'd learnt a lot from him. He may not have had *The Talk* and we weren't really suited, but I had been part of a conversation that had changed my outlook on something, and that is a really valuable thing.

So how do you find out whether he or she has *The Talk*?

Questions! Ask questions when you are on a date. Don't just talk about yourself. Be interested in the other person. Find out what they think about life, God, their family and friends. Find out what their favourite colour is, their favourite item of clothing or type of cheese, whether they would eat chocolate or crisps, which country they would most like to visit. It sounds really geeky, but you could even think of the questions before your date.

One of my favourite date questions is 'What three absolutely-necessary-to-happiness things do you do every day, which you feel sad if you don't do?' Mine are: give someone a hug (not always possible, but it can be a virtual hug in the form of a kind word or a compliment), sing (even if quietly under my breath) and eat chocolate (even if only a small amount). Think of a few questions like this and you should get some interesting conversation going.

Of all the dates I went on the ultimate user of questions was a guy called Simon who I talk about a bit later. He asked a lot of questions from the outset and they were sweet, disarming and beguiling. Questions like 'What is your favourite cake?', 'Have you ever broken any bones?', 'What makes you smile?' and 'Which bearded celebrity would you most like to hug?' They showed me that Simon was genuinely interested in getting to know me. The questions also revealed quite a lot about Simon's own character and personality.

Strong stuff: They say that there are three things you shouldn't talk about at a polite dinner party: sex, politics and religion. I've always thought this was a shame, as these often make for the most interesting conversations. I think that it can be OK to discuss controversial subjects on a first date, but then I was brought up to like a good debate. You may, or may not, wish to test out the water with a few of the following:

- Your faith – this one is pretty simple – you are probably going to want to discuss this. It might be simple for your date as well, or not, depending on whether they are of the same persuasion.
- Your political leanings – better to find out now if they are a raving Tory or a loony Leftie and whether you match up.
- Your views on hot topics: evolution, abortion, homosexuality – go on – I dare you!
- War and peace – what do you think as a Christian?
- Fairtrade, justice, vegetarianism, hunting – the list goes on . . .

It's definitely best not to be too strident or forceful on a first date

Of course, if you disagree on something, it doesn't mean that you are incompatible. Iron sharpens iron, and you could learn something from another point of view. It is very important to come across as open minded and willing to listen if you do get onto hot topics.

However, it's definitely best not to be too strident or forceful on a first date. Be yourself, but don't launch into a self-righteous rant about the rights of the mongoose in Outer Mongolia. If your date doesn't happen to share your strong feelings on the subject they may well feel under attack and react badly (so they are ignorant of mongoose rights – is that really their fault?!). Although, at least if you test these controversial waters early on you will know their point of view. So if you decide that mongoose rights are so important to you that your date's lack of dedication to mongooses (or mongai?) means you could never love them, then you never have to see them again and you can politely decline a second date.

It's probably also best to mix the serious and the light-hearted on a first date. You are just feeling your way and testing out the water, seeing what this person is all about. You are not trying to change their world view.

Subjects to avoid: Although bravery and risk taking are fun in conversation, there are a few areas that I would definitely stay well clear of at all costs on a first date. Here they are, in no particular order:

- Your own sex life (if you have had one) – really not appropriate at this stage.
- Marriage – definitely not appropriate at this stage.
- Former relationships – it is a very bad move to spend your first date with someone cataloguing all your former relationships, especially if done in a bitter way. One of my friends went on a date with a man who did exactly this, and when she complained he said that he was only telling her all the shortcomings of his former girlfriends so that she would feel good about herself in comparison! She told him it had backfired and refused to see him again. The only exception to this rule is that it is a good idea to say if you have been divorced, as this is something that may affect how your date views you and should be brought out in an honest way as early as possible.
- Any person you have not forgiven – whether it is a former lover, or your mother, please, please don't do yourself the disservice of coming across as bitter or full of hate. If there's someone you haven't yet forgiven in your life, don't bring them up on a first date.

Finding common ground: It is wise to be sensitive on a first date. If you see the other person's eyes glazing over, you might want to stop talking about the national cheese rolling championships, the stock exchange or whatever you have been talking about for the last half an hour. Likewise, you should only take your polite interest so far. Try to give some small indication that building models from matchsticks is not your favourite pastime, or that Take That do not rock your world, and never did. Otherwise, you could find yourself trapped in a relationship where you have to pretend to be interested in rearranging your sock drawer just to keep up appearances.

Don't whine and moan: If you are not generally a self-pitying person, why behave like one on a first date? Some people seem to think sob stories are a good tactic to get people to like you. One word: no! Being positive, chirpy and together is far more attractive than making yourself out to be a loser.

Don't boast: You will not endear yourself to anyone.

Your job: This is a good one. Although 'what do you do?' is a very time-worn phrase, it is of interest. You spend on average 40 per cent of your waking hours at your job, so in many senses it is an important part of who you are. It's best to remember here as well that all work has value – don't be snooty or elitist, and you might be pleasantly surprised.

Travel: Another good one. It can show you are adventurous, broad minded and interesting. Best not to hint about holiday destinations for you as a couple just yet though . . .!

Hobbies: A classic. Just don't expect to have the same ones, and be prepared to listen to tales of their hobbies as well as listing your own exploits at the Berkshire medieval re-enactment jousting tournament.

Families: Yes, this can be good. It's always good to know how many siblings your date has but don't intimidate them by naming a fifty-strong clan; and don't let any rancour or bitterness creep in when discussing gruesome Auntie Susan. Families can do strange things to us, and turn us into creatures that we are not. Be wary.

And finally . . . probably the worst thing I have ever been asked by a man:

A particularly sensitive topic of conversation is that of body shape and size. I was once asked by a particularly skinny man one of the worst questions I have ever been asked: 'Can you feel your fat?'

I think he was genuinely interested to know how it feels to have a bit of fat, never having experienced it for himself. Now I'm not enormously fat, but yes – I do have a bit of a spare tyre, as many of us do – especially around Christmas time. Can I feel it? Yes, I suppose I can. I am aware that it is there. I try to keep it under control, but I also try to love it, because what else can you do when you love chocolate as much as I do?

I was once asked by a particularly skinny man one of the worst questions I have ever been asked: 'Can you feel your fat?'

Guys – if you are skinny, never, ever ask the above question – even if you are genuinely interested in how it feels to be fat.

It will not produce a positive response.

The Joy of Texts?

While we are on the subject of poor communication, I must bring up the subject of the serial texter. This is someone who uses texting as a way to hide and not reveal themselves. They will text and text for ages, and you never actually get to hear a human voice. It is very unsatisfactory, and can be surprisingly common. One of my twenty dates was a serial texter called Emmanuel, and I got quite tired of seeing 'Imma' pop up on my phone screen next to a little picture of an envelope. Over-text is rather more common as a male characteristic in the early days (sorry, guys, but you know it's true), and it may be up to the girl to prod her man over the hurdle of this shortcut dating technique.

This type of techno-dating is not limited to texting; it also applies to Facebook, email, MSN, Twitter, Skype, etc.

Of course, texting is a great way to let someone know that you are thinking of them or to make practical arrangements. But if it's all you are giving to the other person then there's something very wrong. It smacks of a lack of commitment, and not wanting to get to know the other person in a real way. Worse, it can be used as a method of running away and not taking responsibility for the fact that you are two actual people in a real-life setting, not just fingers at the end of a phone.

Of course techno-dating is completely unsustainable in a proper grown-up relationship. Just think about it for a moment, and imagine how it would be if people conducted serious romances purely by text:

'I think u are gr8!'

'Really? Me 2!!! (I mean I think U are gr8 – not me! Soz!)'

'I thnk I am falling in luv w u. What wud I do w-out u? Lol!'

'2nite is a very special nite. I want 2 ask u sthing v imp. Will u marry me? ☺'

'U may now X th bride.' (That's the vicar texting there by the way.)

Apologies to all the dudes who think that texting is an acceptable way to conduct their relationships, but just picture a marriage where texting was the chief form of communication. It culminates in the ultimate unsuitable text conversation:

'How wuz it 4u darling? Wuz gr8 4 me.'

Or even worse:

'Not 2nite dear. I hv a hdache. ☹'

You can't negotiate by text, you can't resolve arguments, or really apologize

You can't negotiate by text, you can't resolve arguments, or really apologize, without looking into the other person's eyes. You can't discuss a book you've just read or the news. You can't tell a decent joke. You cannot converse!

So it seems pretty clear texting is not a good way to conduct your relationship. But the question remains:

How do you convert a serial texter into a caller?

If you find yourself in the serial text situation with your current love interest, I suggest you try texting them one of the following messages to get them to raise the stakes and actually give you a call:

'I would love to hear your voice again.'

'Can't text now – busy at work. Let's talk later?'

'Lovely to hear from you. Speak soon.' (Hint hint.)

'I have arthritis in my thumbs and cannot text at great length. Give me a call!'

By sending one of these messages, or a version of them, you will be making it clear that, as good as texting is, you also need voice and face-to-face communication too.

And from the other side . . . of course it's nerve-wracking the first time you call that new special person in your life. You may get flashbacks to being young and calling your first sweetheart. You can't see the person's face and read all those non-verbal signals. But it really is a step that you must take, otherwise you will never get anywhere. Overcome your fear – step out of your comfort zone and call – you may be surprised by just how much more rich and fulfilling a conversation is than a text.

So seize that phone and get your texting fingers ready to dial a number. Apart from anything else, you don't get repetitive strain syndrome from talking (at least, I've never heard of it).

How many kisses?

Oh, and one more thing about text messaging. Don't get hung up on kisses – whether to put them, how many to put, what their significance is. If you text with a kiss and you don't get one back it doesn't mean he or she doesn't love you. Maybe the best thing is to give them a call. That way you'll soon find out what they're really thinking.

8

DATING NITTY GRITTY!

'A very small degree of hope is sufficient to cause the birth of love'
– Stendhal

Where to?

So now you have asked someone out and they have said yes. It took a lot of effort – maybe all the strength you thought you could muster; but being brave enough to ask someone on a date is just the beginning. The first question you need to ask yourself is where should you go? Going for dinner and drinks is the usual first date routine; but how about doing something a little more adventurous and exciting, something that will make your first meeting extra-special and memorable. You could . . .

- ♥ Go to the local park and play on the swings and roundabouts. Buy an ice cream and see who can finish theirs last.
- ♥ Go to the zoo. It's probably been a while since you did. Or if you are feeling adventurous visit a safari park . . . or the Natural History Museum in London.
- ♥ Visit a comedy club – laughter is a great bonder and gets the endorphins flowing!

- Go to an old-fashioned sweet shop and buy all the things that you used to have as a kid – flying saucers, sherbet fountains, Millions, sherbet pips, aniseed balls, push pops – then find a sunny spot and eat them all in one sitting. Enjoy the sugar high!
- Go to a theme park or a fair ground. Go on everything and make yourself feel more alive.
- Go and see a live band. Be daring – go and see some jazz or classical!
- Go to a castle or abbey. Take a picnic and sit in the grounds having a quiet afternoon in the sun. Take some bread to feed the ducks as well.
- Row, row, row your boat gently down the river or round the lake. Boats are cheap to hire for an hour or so. Take a book of poems, jokes or short stories to read to the rower.
- If, like me, you have misspent rather a lot of time at university, you could go to a snooker or pool hall, or rack up a few games in your local pub.
- Go to an old-style art deco cinema if there is one in your area. It's more special than the multiplex.
- Visit an art gallery or museum. They are often cheap or free.

And if you are looking for something even more unusual you could . . .

- Go fishing! Or failing that, buy some goldfish and a tank to keep them in . . . or have a fish and chip supper. Whichever you prefer!

There are only two places that I would say are completely out of bounds for a first, second or third date: one is home – yours or his; the other is your church. Home is a bad plan for many reasons that I won't go into here, but the chief one is covered in chapter 15. As for your church, an early date there would just be weird. It is much too soon to be introducing him or her to your friends because you are still just getting to know the person. Introducing your date to all your friends, relations and the vicar probably isn't the best idea – especially if you bring another date along three weeks later, and another three weeks after that. Do you see where I'm headed with this?

As for your church, an early date there would just be weird

So unless you both go to the same church anyway, stay out of the building until date four – after that, go wild if you like!

Should you go on a second date?

Yes! You may be surprised by how quickly I have answered in the affirmative, but my advice would definitely be to give him or her at least two chances, if not three. You may have felt only lukewarm on the first date but things might improve as your date relaxes and the nerves on both sides disappear. If they still aren't doing it for you after three dates I would probably call it a day.

Of course, if your first date was an absolute disaster then you are under no obligation at all to meet up again. However, definitions of 'disaster' can vary massively. Some people think that a 'disaster' means that you didn't like the shirt that your date was wearing, or that you didn't enjoy the food at the restaurant, or that you felt silly. I would encourage you to think a little more broadly and focus on who the person is, rather than the undercooked pizza or the fact that it was a little awkward because it was a first date.

If you are having trouble deciding whether to go on that second date you could try creating a Date Disaster checklist to help you make your mind up. Here is a quick quiz to assess your date's disastrousness:

- Were they on time? Yes/No
- Were they easy to talk to? Yes/No
- Did you have interesting things to talk about together? Yes/No
- Did time fly past, or did it feel as though it was dragging? Yes, it flew/No, it dragged
- Did they make you laugh? Yes, like a drain/No, their attempts to do so made me cringe/No, they didn't even try to make me laugh
- Did you make them laugh? Yes, uproariously/No, though I tried all my best jokes
- Were they polite to you? Yes/No
- Did they seem kind and affectionate? Did they talk about other people – friends and family – in an affectionate way? Yes/No
- Were they respectful (no physical boundaries crossed which shouldn't have been crossed on a first date)? Yes/No

  Were you attracted to them? Yes/No
- Did they treat other people (e.g. waiters) with respect? Yes/No
- Did you think about them the next day? Yes/No

If you answer 'yes' to four or more of these questions then you should go for that second and third date and give them another try, even if you have reservations. You may find that they grow on you. If the answer is 'no' to more than eight, you should probably steer clear of seeing them again, as there are just too many negatives.

How do you let someone down gently after three dates?

If you decide after three dates that you and this new person are not compatible, you are going to have to let them know.

This is a tricky one, especially if they have allowed the relationship to get a lot bigger in their heads than it is in reality. Most of us have been there, on both sides, at one time or another, so we can totally sympathize with the person we are about to hurt. And yet it must be done, because it would be far worse to let the thing drag out and hurt them even more as a result.

It would be far worse to let the thing drag out and hurt them even more as a result

The best way to break it off with someone you have been seeing is face to face. The second best way is over the phone. Never have this conversation by email, and definitely, definitely never by text message. I have been disposed of by text message once before and it really is the most insulting thing to experience.

Also, don't start bringing God into it at this stage, or using God as a shield or 'excuse' to hide behind. Even if you genuinely feel that God is telling you not to be with this person, it is going to be a very uncomfortable and difficult thing for that person to hear, especially if they have heard otherwise. So the respectful thing to do is to explain that you don't think you have a future together, and that you would rather end it now than later.

There are a few things it is best not to say:

'It's not you, it's me.'

This comes across as insincere and it is such a cliché.

'I just don't feel that I'm ready for another relationship after my last one.'

Although this is an easy and apparently un-hurtful way to tell someone you don't want to take things any further, it is best not to use it unless you are absolutely 100 per cent sure that this is the case. This is especially true if you are likely to start seeing someone else within a few weeks. It is going to be so much more painful for the other person when they find out that you were lying.

'I'm sure you will find someone soon.'

This just sounds patronizing.

It's always good to say something positive if you can; like 'I've enjoyed the time we have spent together', or 'I think you are a great person', before you say the big 'but'.

Remember, you have the right to call a halt to the relationship at any time during these early stages. You don't owe the other person anything. You have not made a commitment, or got married yet. Whatever you do, don't let a short relationship continue out of obligation to the other person. This is not a good basis for a relationship. It honours the other person far better to get out at an early stage, giving them the chance to find someone who loves them completely and wholeheartedly. They deserve that, and so do you.

PART II

STEADY

In which some potential traps and pitfalls of dating are explored, and the need for you to be aware and steer clear of these is explained

9

SLOWING IT DOWN AND BEING ON THE SAME PAGE

'In the morning, O LORD . . . I lay my requests before you and wait in expectation'
– Psalm 5:3

Have you ever had the situation where you have been on a couple of dates with someone – things are going well, you are getting to know them and you like what you are getting to know. Then BLAM! Out of nowhere, they drop a bombshell and you suddenly realize that they are thinking totally differently to you about the 'relationship' you have? Not only are you not on the same page, you are not even reading the same chapter. He or she – the lovely guy or gal you were just getting to know – is actually a whole half-book ahead of you at least.

Take the example of Eduardo. I met up with him a couple of times and we really enjoyed ourselves. The first time we went out for drinks and a meal. The conversation flowed well, we had loads in common and we put the world to rights. The second we went to the theatre to see a really excellent play (his choice, I was impressed). Now, at the time I met up with him I was in a particularly busy patch – things were manic at work and I was about to be

Boy, was that a freak-out moment

a bridesmaid for my friend, so it was difficult to find the time to arrange anything. Nonetheless, I was enjoying gradually getting to know him and I thought the same was true with him. So we were merrily texting back and forth, happy light-hearted things.

And then, suddenly the bombshell from him:

'Well, I don't know about you but meeting up with someone once a month isn't my idea of happiness.'

Boy, was that a freak-out moment. Suddenly I was responsible for this man's *happiness*! I barely knew him . . . Surely he could look after himself a little better than this? Suddenly I could feel the weight of responsibility on my shoulders, weighing me down. He wanted to see me a *lot* or he wouldn't be happy. I had to make room for him in my life *now*, or I was going to lose him. This was the message he was giving, even if he didn't mean to. And the threat of losing him? Well, it didn't really distress me because we had only been on two dates. How could I miss him when I didn't know him at all? While we should have been keeping the balance, he had totally lost it and descended into neediness.

Well, what could I do?

I had to break it off – I simply didn't feel I could meet his needs.

The sad thing is, I actually really quite liked the guy and it might have gone somewhere, but by going for the jugular like that so early on he destroyed it in one.

I'm not saying that once you are in a committed, long-term relationship you shouldn't make time for each other – of course you should. But in the very early days, please keep calm, for everyone's sake!

Unfortunately, I have also been the perpetrator in this scenario at times, freaking out under the pressure of all those early questions in my own brain, trying to speed the other person on to the finish line and completely putting them off instead. It is embarrassing some of the things I have allowed myself to think and then act on . . . and all of it completely counter-productive.

So what can you do if you are the type to obsess about someone prematurely? Here's a three-step process that you can follow to stop yourself ruining something good (I use this all the time!):

1) Remind yourself that they are human and are busy people.
2) Remind yourself that if you *don't* end up with this particular person it is not the end of the world.
3) Remind yourself that you have an important and fun life (see chapter 16), then get back out there and LIVE IT! Visit an old friend for coffee, call your mum, go to work, for a walk, or to your choir practice. Go clubbing and have a few drinks if need be! Whatever you do, be dignified (so not too many drinks) and keep perspective! You have far too many other things going on in your fabulous life to be obsessively worrying about a particular person who is a relatively new part of it – trust me on this one . . . You will find out it is true as soon as they run away after you freak out. Suddenly the ordinary perspective of life will return and you will wonder what on earth you were thinking.

If you find this particularly problematic, ask a friend to help you out. Get them to be a safety valve – the person you call if you feel the fear creeping up on you. Then take a deep breath and be sane with the object of your affection.

You can actually feel the wrinkles gathering as you wait for the confirmation

What if you have the opposite problem, and things seem to be inching along and barely progressing at all? You can actually feel the wrinkles gathering as you wait for the confirmation that yes, this is a relationship and it is going to go somewhere. This could mean one of two things:

1) There is a problem. This person does not really want to be with you and they are trying to keep you at arm's length and think of ways to let you down gently. Or they are afraid of making a commitment.

Or

2) They are just getting to know you and you are panicking unnecessarily. You need to calm down and let things progress at a natural pace.

Take careful stock of your situation and assess whether you are over-reacting. Nine times out of ten it is more likely to be (2) than (1), and what does it matter anyway? Why are you in such a hurry? Remember, you have a life that you love (chapter 16 again) and your Mr or Miss Right is going to have to take the time to join in and become part of your life, eventually (perhaps) a very important part of it.

Give it time and it may well happen naturally – it might not, but whatever you do don't push things along by being over-eager or downright weird. After all – you want to be with someone who actually wants to be with you – you don't want to constantly have the thought in the back of your mind that you have pushed, hurried and harassed this person into being with you. Even if they think you are fab, coercion is never the best basis for a relationship.

The fact is that you are going to have to live in the discomfort of Not Knowing for a while . . . It is all part of forming a relationship and *most dates will not turn into a relationship*. Once you know these two facts you can breathe a big sigh of relief and get on with enjoying getting to know your new person.

If none of this works, and you are still struggling to push the relationship, maybe you should think again about whether you want to be with this person . . . After all, the love of your life won't make you feel panicky, will they?

Top dating tip: SLOW DOWN! Get someone to help you if needed. However you do it, put the brakes onto your skiddy heart and get it under control – it will be worth it in the long run!

10

NEEDINESS

'The foolish man seeks happiness in the distance, the wise grows it under his feet'
– James Oppenheim

There is a saying about love, and it goes like this: 'Take hold tightly – let go lightly.'

Now I am not sure that I entirely agree with this sentiment.

In one sense, yes – it is good to take hold tightly. If you like someone you should give your whole self to them and vice-versa. But not too much too soon! Whether you are 3 days, 3 weeks or 3 months into a relationship you are not yet a married couple and (in most cases – not all, but most) you should not really be contemplating anything like that situation with this particular person.

Meet Molly, Zeb, Sarah and Mark

Molly: 'I don't understand what's gone wrong. I just don't get it. Zeb and I were getting on so well. At first I wasn't too sure about him, but then on the third date I suddenly got it. I thought – yes, I like this guy – he is the one. So I started letting my guard down a bit. You know, telling him how I feel, giving him a ring now and then. And then suddenly everything went quiet on his end. It's like all those things he said were just lies – he just seemed to go right off me with no good reason. So I told him the problem – how I feel – and the next thing I know – I'm dumped. Men!'

She kept ringing at bizarre times. She texted about 10 times a day – at least

Zeb: 'I don't understand what's gone wrong. I just don't get it. We were getting on so well. It was going great at first. Molly seemed really cool – feisty, funny, independent. But then on the third date she suddenly flipped. I got busy with work so I couldn't call her for a few days and it's like she completely changed personality. She kept ringing me at bizarre times. She texted about 10 times a day – at least. I felt stressed out and guilty 'cause I couldn't call her back. I just had to get out – it was too much too soon. Looking back, she was cool, but what could I do? Women!'

Sarah: 'Mark was really lovely on the date. We got on really well. I'm not sure that I fancied him that much but I was definitely keen for another meet up. But then he started acting really strange. He would text me really weird stuff at all times of the night. So I backed off.'

Mark: 'Sarah's the one. I just know it. I knew as soon as I looked at her. God spoke to me and said, "This is it,

Mark." So I didn't hold back – I told her. But she heard something different apparently. One of us must have heard wrong. I'm sure it wasn't me.'

The mists of neediness have descended and it is really not a good place to be for either party. Neediness is a stage up from being on a different page. It is an overwhelming need to Define the Relationship (DtR) and know exactly where it is going very early on. See if you recognize these symptoms:

- You over-analyse every text message trying to figure out what they are thinking.
- You think about them every two minutes.
- You feel panicky, powerless and out of control.
- You can't sleep, eat, think or concentrate.
- You are 'in agony'.

If you have any or all of the above symptoms for any length of time then you have entered a very bad dating zone – it is called the Needy Frightened Zone and it is not good.

Needy is not attractive. Needy is not sexy. Needy is not cool. Needy might be just a little bit crazy.

OK, honesty time. Does any of this sound familiar? It does to me! This feeling of being infatuated and afraid that it isn't reciprocated is a bit like drowning. You are in the situation of inwardly obsessing about someone, but not really thinking about *them* at all. When you are being needy you don't think about the person as an individual – only about the idea you have of them . . . and what you believe they can do for you: fill a hole or a gap, provide kids, make you feel like you are loved and belong. Because it does become all about you when you are in the Needy Zone, this is not good for anyone!

I experienced this condition about four years ago with a guy called Mike. I seemed to be losing my mind. I had fallen for Mike so hard that I didn't know whether I was coming or going – my days revolved around hearing from him – my ears constantly straining for the 'bleep' that would indicate I had received a text. The funny thing about this state of affairs is that when Mike finally dumped me the temporary insanity passed and I felt totally released. The real Becky seemed to wake from a stupor, shake her head, blink and resume her normal place. After just a couple of months I was able to look at Mike quite rationally, see that he was a perfectly nice bloke but that we weren't suited at all. He really wasn't worth getting so worked up over.

Vanquishing neediness

If you find you are sinking into the panic of 'Does he like me? Doesn't he? Why doesn't he call?' or 'Why can't I be with her? She's perfect. I deserve her. Why isn't God giving me someone I deserve?' I'll tell you what I have learned you should take hold tightly of: the Saviour. Hold his hand tightly and don't let go. He will pull you out of the water and into a much better, clearer place. I heard about one woman who whenever she felt the neediness creeping would take it as an invitation from God to draw closer to him. Instead of running to the man she was currently interested in for affirmation and love, she would use it as an opportunity to speak to her heavenly Father. She said it wasn't easy at first, but in the discipline of it she found a freedom. She said it reminded her that although people will let you down God never will – he is eternal and unchanging. He knows the plans he has for you. So trust in that and be content that he will answer your prayers in his time and the way he wants to.

I believe neediness is one of the biggest relationship killers in the church today

This doesn't mean that you sit back and do nothing – quite the opposite. I think God wants you to be proactive about finding your soul mate, but he wants you to do it with a contented and confident heart.

I believe neediness is one of the biggest relationship killers in the church today and we have got to beat this attack. And I knew I was never going to beat it by looking to another person for blame or absolution. It begins and ends with two things: me and God.

He's in charge. If he guides you away from a person you thought you loved then so be it. If he guides you towards them then so be it as well.

He's in control. Just three words, but so powerful. Every day I'm still trying to live like they are true.

Letters I never sent

While we are on the subject of stormy emotions, I'd like to bring up the subject of letters, and suggest that you think very hard before you send someone a love letter. Remember that the sentiments, thoughts and feelings that you express on paper will last forever for that person. To them, the words will be indelible truth – even when you have long since forgotten the letter's content. And they might interpret the words differently to you. They will be able to go back and read those words again and again so that nothing has changed in their mind, even if it has in yours. By all means write the letters if they relieve your feelings, but do consider carefully whether it might be best not to send them. Every time I have decided not to send a letter like that I have been relieved that I didn't. Somewhere in my teenage (and early twenties!) relics there is a box full of letters I never sent – the impulsive ramblings of a young, romantic fool. Those letters will never see the light of day because they all express the passing feelings of a moment – not the lasting feelings of real love. And looking back, I'm very glad that I kept them to myself.

Women's issues?

I have heard it said that it is in a woman's nature to be needy sometimes; that women are instinctively more caring, compulsive and generous with their love. I don't think this is necessarily true. Apart from anything else it would be insulting a man's capacity for love to say so.

What I do believe is that women are more conditioned to act in this over-romantic manner early on in a relationship which can come across as nutty. The whole female world is geared more to talking about feelings and expressing them as and when you feel them. So where a man might clam up and keep his burgeoning emotions to himself, a woman will let rip and perhaps say more than she means – which can be misinterpreted. It's an age-old problem and one that crops up in the Bible too.

'Daughters of Jerusalem, I charge you: Do not arouse or awaken love until it so desires.'

The Beloved in Song of Songs 8:3 warns her friends of this danger of hurrying things – she does it three times in fact, in exactly the same words. You cannot push a person into the place you want them to be. They must arrive there in their own time. If you let love grow naturally, you too will come up from the desert leaning on your lover.

Not so manic now

If you are on the receiving end of strong neediness early on in a relationship, try to understand that it might be that the person is caught up in the moment and saying more than he or she means. Try to keep seeing the person for who they really are, and if you like the person, don't run away. The chances are that the neediness might fade once he or she realizes you are not going anywhere, and are not perfect anyway – so be a little understanding if you can. I haven't always managed this myself (see Eduardo in the last chapter), but I will try to be more understanding if it happens again in the future.

And if you are the one being needy – try to keep it under control! Be honest about your feelings, yes, but try to think how what you say comes across. I've seen it from both sides and it can be awkward. Neediness doesn't inspire love, just pity. I know it's difficult to keep from blurting out an emotion as you feel it – those emotions are powerful things. But try using your head as well as your heart. Ultimately, just trust in something, take it a day at a time, and above all relax – it will come right in the end.

And if you are the one being needy – try to keep it under control!

The power of choice

Emotions are a bit of a minefield in some ways – at once essential to a good relationship, yet potentially sabotaging if they get out of control. Neediness is one of the less beautiful emotions, and it is a long way from love. Need is about 'me', love is about 'the other'.

Ultimately I think love is about something much more mature and selfless than need. It is about choice: choosing not to be needy; choosing each other; choosing to do [illegible]ings to make your spouse's life a little better and [illegible] – not just once, but every day for as long as you [illegible] it is like following God – a day-by-day deci[illegible] it is not a selfish flitting from one person to anoth[illegible], following whoever might come along next for a while then dropping them. Once you are committed there is a lot of work to be done – but in almost all cases it will be worth it – the invested time, energy and thought. What's better to hear than 'I need you, I just can't help loving you' . . . how about: 'I choose you', 'Out of all the people I have met, I *choose* to love you and be good to you.'

Feelings fade. But love is the decision to devote yourself to another and sticking with that choice. Maybe it is not always easy, but I have heard that the rewards can be beyond measure. One day I'd like to try it!

11

BACHELORS AND SINGLETONS

'He who finds a wife finds what is good and receiv
from the L*ORD'*
– Proverbs 18:22

There are two imaginary made-up characters in this chapter. Their names are Tim and Mim.

Tim is a bachelor.

In Victorian times he would have been known as a 'dandy' – a 'man about town' – debonair, maybe ne'er do well, but always carefree. He is on the brink of 40 and his hair is starting to show steely grey tips. He lives either with his mum, or in a Bachelor Pad – a scrupulously clean modern flat, high up in the air, full of gadgets, gizmos, leather furniture and red wine. It is sort of like Batman's Cave without the Batmobile (or Robin). Tim spends many evenings on his own way up in the sky playing Guitar Hero. Other evenings he is hanging out

A Toxic Tim can be dangerous to girls in their twenties

with the younger men from church or work downtown. Or he is with his latest girlfriend, who won't last longer than two months.

There are many Tims at church, loitering in the corners.

All of us know a Tim or two.

Maybe you are one. Or you have a bit of him in you.

A few of the Tims are Toxic, or going that way. A Toxic Tim can be dangerous to girls in their twenties. He has a habit of letting them fall in love with him, and pretending not to notice until it is too late. Because he is still handsome in a George Clooney way, this happens quite frequently. Like bad apples in a barrel, the Toxic Tims can turn all the other apples bad as well.

But most of the Tims are good people. A good Tim has a lot going for him – he has an excellent job and is now at a stage of the career ladder that is satisfying and well paid, he has wide circles of friends and interests – sports, music, films, gadgets – and yet he feels at sea: adrift without an anchor. He left his adolescence and twenties behind ages ago, but is not quite sure where he is headed. He is just not quite sure what he is *for* any more . . . He might say to a friend (and these are the true words of someone I know):

'I woke up one day and I was 30, then I woke up one day and I was 40. Still no partner, no kids. Time is just slipping away.'

Now meet Tim's counterpart – Mim.

Mim is a singleton.

In Victorian times she would have been known as a 'spinster' or an 'old maid' but these days her title is a bit more positive. At least 'singleton' only sounds desperate rather than hopeless. Mim is in her late thirties but still very attractive. She has an excellent job which she excels at and enjoys. She involves herself in many activities –

church and non-church. She is always busy – perhaps to drown out the ticking of the Clock (she often feels like Captain Hook being followed by the crocodile). The younger women in the church look up to her as profound or spiritual. She is widely travelled, widely read, deep in her walk with God – she has seen a lot of life and she knows exactly who she is.

There are many Mims at church, mingling with groups of single girls of rapidly decreasing age.

All of us know a Mim or two.

Maybe we are one.

Some of the Mims are growing angry deep down, or even bitter. Although they try not to let it show it can slip out at times, especially when they are talking to attractive men.

But most of the Mims are contented people, who like their lives. They are just that little bit lonely, and have a nagging feeling that something is missing. And then there is that darned Clock to contend with – it just keeps ticking away incessantly day and night. Also there are so many babies around – has anyone else noticed all the babies at every turn?

❖ ❖ ❖

She is so beautiful.
And such a Godly lady

And what are the Tims and Mims doing about their sense of being lonely or adrift?

Well, I'm sorry to say that some of them are falling in love with the most inappropriate people!

For example, Tim is actually 'in love' with

Sarah, who is just 20. He reasons with himself – 'at least she isn't a teenager. And she is so beautiful. And such a Godly lady.' So even while Tim is resignedly going on dates with other women – some of whom are actually close in age to him – he cannot shake off the sense that Sarah is the one for him, and can't get anywhere with these other ladies as a result.

And Mim? Mim has fallen for Gabriel, the worship leader who is over here from New Zealand. He has only been here for a month, and has just five months remaining, and they have only exchanged a few platitudes at coffee time. But already she feels a deep spiritual connection with him. He is just so Godly, so creative, so in love with the Lord, and so beautiful with that floppy brown fringe and baby face. He may be ten years younger than her, but Mim is sure that they will connect in a way that will mean that the age gap won't matter, once they have actually spent some time together.

How are either of these two crushes realistically going to develop or go anywhere serious? Maybe occasionally it will work, but as a general rule – no.

Mim and Tim are caricatures of course, but there is an element of truth within these stereotypes.

I think it's time for all of us to take a careful look at ourselves. Of course you must be physically attracted to the person you are with – ideally you should be wild about them. But if you have loads of wrinkles and they don't have a single one then you may need to think again. There are exceptions to this, of course. Some excellent matches are made between people of very different ages. But be honest with yourself about whether the object of your affection is really likely to reciprocate. Then take a good long look in the mirror (and at your birth certificate) and try to aim for someone who is vaguely close to you in age – for your own dignity if for nothing else.

Perfection?

Of course, the impossible search goes beyond looks. Some people seem to be looking for a standard of perfection in their partner that is impossible to reach. For example, must haves:

- A deep, close walk with God
- The ability to play at least one instrument
- Knowledge of political issues
- Buys eco-friendly brands
- Is well travelled, but has not yet visited Indonesia (so that you can go together there on mission after seven months of courtship, where you will also get engaged and set up a project to help children living on the streets . . .)

Do you see where I'm going with this?

A wise man once told me that nobody is perfect in this world; but in a relationship we can learn to be perfect for each other – if we just decide to focus on the other.

So if you meet someone you think is perfect, then it turns out they have certain flaws (and I guarantee you, they will), do not run away. Reassess the situation and decide whether you can live with that flaw or not, then make a decision accordingly.

For example: if you find out that they happen to like *Star Wars*, golf or stamp collecting, then you should probably stick with them – they may be a bit of a geek, but they still have all the other amazing qualities that you are falling in love with (and anyway, geekiness is endearing).

Keep your sense of proportion and realize that you are not going to share everything in common and that this is a *good thing*. Think how boring it would be otherwise!

Don't be a Mim or a Tim – be prepared to compromise – it may be the best thing you ever do!

Serial monogamy

The other mistake that is often made by Mims and Tims is serial monogamy. This is having one long-term partner for two or more years, then waiting till it fizzles out, breaking up with them and finding a new one. Two years later the same thing happens again, and so on ad infinitum. Most of these relationships should have ended much earlier than they did, but they somehow dragged on.

I have one word for you if you are a Serial Monogamist: Matrimony!

Seriously, you are old enough by now to step up to the plate and decide to commit. As a Mim or a Tim you have sown your wild oats, made your hay, had your cake and eaten it (all in the metaphorical sense of course). To put it briefly, you have lived enough to know who you are and what you want, and to know that sometimes you need to just take the plunge.

Also, it is a really good and positive thing that you have reached this more mature stage before thinking about getting married. You will know a lot more about yourself now than you did at 20, and will be far better prepared for the difficulties that may arise.

So, if not now then when, Mr and Ms Prevaricator? Pop the question!

You have lived enough to know who you are and what you want

Zimmer frames

The ultimate conclusion of carrying on like Tim and Mim with our crazy crushes and prevarication is that we are still going to be single in the old folks' home. We will be there, wobbling around on our Zimmer frames and mentally rejecting the other old folk who definitely don't measure up to our standards with their sags and wrinkles, whilst completely failing to notice that we are saggy and wrinkly ourselves.

Think about it – Tim and Mim should be on their tandem Zim at the end of a long happy life together; instead they are wobbling around on their own . . . It is actually tragic. Don't let it happen!

So what if you are not a Tim or Mim?

What if you are not fussy, or picky, or afraid to pop the question? What if you are one of those whose only standard is that the other person must have some hair somewhere on their body and some teeth – their own preferred, but you will settle for false ones quite happily. What if you are one of those who has had a long and lonely wait for love and you can't see any light at the end of the tunnel?

Ask yourself whether you have really actively tried every possible avenue to find that special person? It might be that God wants you to take some action before your heart's desire is fulfilled.

You may be one of those servant-hearted people who spend all their time doing things to help, running after others, cooking, cleaning, putting out chairs at church. There are always one or two people like this in most situations (not least church) – those who are always helping, in any event, at any time of the day or night. And they are usually single and without family – which is why they can spend the time doing these things.

If you are one of those, I reckon that you, Mr or Miss Helpful, are going to make someone very, very happy. You are an incredibly giving and generous person, you are willing to do anything to make another person happy, and that is a great thing to bring to a relationship (within reason – you don't want to be a doormat!). But before you can give yourself generously to someone as you are so capable of doing, you need to do something for yourself. You need to get out there and find someone to love and be loved by. It really isn't selfish to take some time and effort to look for love. Go and get dating!

And if you are already out there looking? Look again at whether you are making any of the mistakes of being too picky, trying to find a standard that doesn't exist, or being unwilling to compromise. If you are not doing any of these things then just keep at it! I truly believe that if you don't give up or become permanently heartbroken or bitter, one day you will meet someone you can have a successful relationship with. They won't be perfect. They may like to iron their underwear or clip their toenails into the sink. But they will still be perfect for you.

12

KILLING THE FANTASY

'Fantasy, abandoned by reason, produces impossible monsters . . .'
– Francisco de Goya

I must admit that I am a perfectionist. I have always been particular about who I go out with, and had high expectations – perhaps unreasonably high. The reason for this is that for a long time I have had a fantasy figure in my head. In my imagination, this man and I will be so attuned, so on the same wavelength, that we will have barely any need for words. Despite this we will have very deep conversations and an intellectual parity. We will make each other laugh all the time yet be able to talk seriously, and we will be deeply attracted to each other. We will want all the same things out of life and want to go to the same places. We will be of the same age and at the same stage in life. We will find favour with each other's families and friends. We will both have excellent jobs and no money worries. In short our relationship will be seamless and smooth and completely obviously right from the first.

If you also believe all these things about your future partner, I have some bad news born from stark experience: it isn't going to happen! There has to be some compromise.

Sure you need to have some of those aspects – and I think you should expect to have some of them, otherwise why would you want to be with the person at all?! But the whole package? You will never find it. Even if you do find that level of perfection, do you think it's likely that they will be living next door to you, or in the same city, or country . . .?

Also, do you think it is likely that you will stay quite so high, so enthusiastic, so crazily in love throughout your entire marriage? An older couple who have been consistently in love since they first met haven't been spending the thirty or forty years that they've been together obsessively wondering what the other person is doing, whether they are thinking about them, what they are wearing, etc. Eventually things will settle down into contentment no matter how fired up you both were at the beginning. You will have jobs and kids and friends and things – you will still have the other person, but whereas before they were your sun, moon and starlit sky, now they are the wonderful backdrop against which and with whom life will be played out. You need to be ready for that, and to see the change from early passion to deep, patient commitment and cherishing as a good thing.

So here's my challenge. If you have a fantasy figure, you need to grab them right now, take them outside and kill them. You need to do it right now because that little fantasy man or woman is spoiling your chance of seizing hold of everything God has in store for you.

For years I was chasing the fantasy man. I would fall for someone inwardly because I found them charming or good-looking; play out a little fantasy about them that was about me really, not the person in question; then be hurt and disappointed when the knock-back came. I spent ages trying to kill my fantasy man, but he plagued me – and sometimes he still does. He kept coming back to life like the monster in a horror movie – popping up in different guises. A few years ago I never recognized him for what he was. I don't blame those men I projected my fantasy onto – but neither do I blame myself. He still pops up sometimes, but nowadays I am able to recognize him instantly and can more or less ignore him. So he has pretty much lost the power he used to have over me. He has become flaccid and impotent and I laugh at him!

Why are we inclined to seek something that doesn't exist? I don't know

Why are we inclined to seek something that doesn't exist? I don't know. There is the romantic comedy argument, which suggests that the schmaltzy, sugary, unrealistic romances that are played out across our screens have warped our view of what a relationship is like. Maybe that is true to an extent. And yet, I can't fully let go of my belief in romantic love because I believe it is the highest expression of God's love for us.

Maybe when it finally happens it just doesn't feel like those romantic fantasies because it is tinged with the mundane or because the romance must be played out alongside all the other aspects of life – hunger, tiredness, work stress and stomach upsets. In the romantic world nothing else matters but the love between the hero and heroine. They live, breathe and exist for one another. There is nothing and no-one but the two of them. However, in the real world we interact with other people or are pulled away from them by circumstance. We must catch buses, pay taxes, open junk mail and clean the toilet. Also, we misunderstand what the other person is saying sometimes, mis-communicate, neglect each other, overlook things. We are not perfect after all.

Have you ever noticed that all romance stories are about the chase, not the reality? Once the hero and heroine fall into each other's arms, the credits roll and that's it – end of film. Any book or film that examines marriage or long-term love is tinged with darkness and sadness. Even if the couple are happy with each other, illness, debt, troubles and death come into their lives. A couple unites against the darkness, but the darkness is still there as well as the light.

The beauty of compromise

Although I don't believe in perfection, I do believe couples can have a deep and sustaining friendship and desire for one another. There can be new things that are fresh each day. There is a different kind of subtlety about a real, long-lasting love. And what about the gracious beauty of the love between a couple who have been together for many years? What about the fact of their time together, their commitment? Their love is played out in shades of grey rather than black and white and it is deeply romantic.

I remember seeing my grandparents, both aged 88 at the time, and happily married for sixty-one years, dancing at my mother's sixtieth birthday party

I remember seeing my grandparents, both aged 88 at the time, and happily married for sixty-one years, dancing at my mother's sixtieth birthday party. They danced alone, taking up the whole dance floor while the guests stood round in a circle, watched and smiled. They didn't mind being the centre of attention – they were happy to show off their love. My grandmother leant against her husband for support. He held her up, occasionally wincing as his back gave a twinge, but visibly enjoying it nonetheless. It was more of a shuffle than a dance really, but it was very beautiful.

It was the last time they were to dance together. My grandmother became ill a few months later and my grandfather now cares for her as best he can. Even in the last years of their life, their relationship has changed again.

People change, and relationships and marriages, no matter how good, are inevitably a series of compromises and adaptations. This is a fact. You only have to think of couples you know to realize how each of them have made certain sacrifices and mutual decisions in order to be together. They are still two individuals – but they are no longer autonomous.

There is a basic beauty and dignity in compromise, and it is the core – even the life blood – of a lifelong relationship. In fact, I would go further and say that life itself – any kind of achievement, any fulfilled ambition or success – is based on compromise.

To illustrate this, think of your greatest achievement to date. Maybe it is a party that you once threw, something you made, somewhere you visited, a job you landed, maybe even your children (if you are at that stage reading this). Do you remember the glow of achievement when you succeeded in reaching your goal? Wasn't it amazing? I bet you felt on top of the world!

Now think of the compromises surrounding this achievement. There are bound to be some. Even if the achievement itself is unsullied by attenuating circumstances, there will be something related that you had to compromise on. For example, maybe in order to do that dream job you had to move to a place that you wouldn't have chosen to live. Maybe in order to complete your magnum opus you had to spend a little less time with your friends. Maybe you had to give up one hobby in order to excel at another.

It might be that the end product is different to how you anticipated it; or things weren't quite how you expected along the way. You had to be brave. Sometimes something didn't work and you had to go back and try a different way.

But in the end it was better than any fantasy, because it was *real*.

I think the same rules apply to lifelong love. It's not going to be the fuzzy, rosy romance that you have carried around in your head for years. There will be things you don't like about your partner, as well as things that you do. You won't have everything in common – there will be some things you share, and some you don't. There will be things that surprise you – some of them wonderfully unexpected, some less wonderful.

If you go marching into the dating scene unprepared to compromise on finding someone who is perfect in your eyes you are really not going to get anywhere.

The other fascinating thing about your greatest achievement is that I bet getting there wasn't really enough. Reaching your goal will have pushed you on to do the next thing, or if there wasn't a 'next thing' you will have been left feeling a little deflated. When you look back, the bits you remember most fondly are those that took you there – the warm glow of the people who helped on the way, the things you learnt about yourself. The great thing about being with someone is that the job is never done. Even after years of being together you will be finding out new things about each other.

The magic screwdriver

As you date and court, you need to remember that you don't have a magic screwdriver that allows you access to your partner's head. You won't be able to open it up whenever you want and snuggle down among all the most secret thoughts of your spouse. You won't know them so well that you feel like one spirit, one body and one brain. That simply doesn't happen.

You can get as close as you can – sharing all sorts of thoughts, ideas and dreams with each other. But your partner will still ultimately be a mystery to you and will remain so for as long as you are together. However, this is where the excitement lies, because it means if you have met someone who you can communicate well with, you will always be finding out new things. This doesn't mean you will never get bored, but it does keep some of the mystery and excitement. How dull would it be if we knew everything that our partner was thinking and feeling?

Your partner will still ultimately be a mystery to you and will remain so for as long as you are together

Learning to be perfect?

I used to have a theory that the person I fall in love with will suit me perfectly in mind, body, heart and soul. Sometimes I still believe that can be the case. I want to be with someone who I can connect with intellectually, who I am attracted to, who will share the kindness and tenderness of his heart, and who will touch me in a way that is beyond explanation and connected to God. On top of this, it will be vice-versa – because I hope to be and do all these things for him!

Is this unrealistic? I don't think so, because I am not expecting this person to be perfect. I have no doubt that there will be things about him that I don't like – habits or preoccupations of mind – and I've no doubt I will annoy and upset him at times too. But we will choose to accept these things and love each other in spite of them, because that is how love is.

So, I have come to the conclusion that there is no such thing as a perfect person; but I do believe that two people can learn to be perfect for each other.

God brings two imperfect people together and they then invest the time, energy, emotion and thought into being perfect for each other. When you see a good marriage, this is what has happened. It is hard work and it takes a lifetime but I'm sure the long-term lovers feel it is worth the effort.

It is a journey I'm ready to start and that's why I decided to date!

'The journey is the destination'

It is a cheesy old saying, but in many ways it is true. Your work of love will never be finished, so for goodness' sake enjoy the scenery as you take the long journey together, and don't make it a race to some kind of finish line – 'marriage' being the most obvious one, but 'going out', 'sex', 'house', 'children', etc. being others. They are all fake finish lines – false summits. Just agree to take the walk of love together for a lifetime, then stick to it. And while you are it, tell the fantasy to get packing.

13

RISKING YOUR HEART

'Love consists in this; that two solitudes protect and touch and greet each other'
– R. Maria Rilke

Earlier I talked about neediness and not coming across as a nutcase (quick question – why is the case of a nut considered crazy? Answers on the back of a postcard please . . .). Leaving aside the origins of nut-casery, I am now going to look at the other side of the neediness question – when it can be right to allow yourself to be vulnerable, and the importance of doing this.

In the church there is often a lot of talk about guarding your heart and keeping it safe. We are admonished to build a protective wall around ourselves, to stay safe from harm. We are encouraged to ask God to help us do this, as though he is in the business of walling up our hearts – shoring them up like a defective sea wall that is letting in the sea.

At first glance, this seems sensible – take it slowly, don't get in too deep, too quickly. Don't let your emotions and your need overtake and lead you into a bad decision. But there is a flaw in this 'softly softly' approach. If we don't allow ourselves to be vulnerable, how can we ever open ourselves up to the possibility of true love when the time is right?

If we are sceptical about things like the Holy Spirit and prayer, we can miss out on so much

It is the same with God's love. If we are sceptical about things like the Holy Spirit and prayer, we can miss out on so much. Also, in my experience, God's love (and love in general) does not respect place, time or person. If God wants you to feel something you are going to feel it.

I've never been very good at opening myself up to God. I tend to take a step back and observe others meeting with him, experiencing him. It can be the same with relationships. I quite often want to take a step back and not engage fully because I am afraid.

It feels like balancing on a tightrope when you are first getting to know and like, then falling in love with someone. You want to allow yourself to be vulnerable and real and open; but you also want to keep a little part of yourself protected 'just in case'. In some ways it is essential to keep this little part protected – for your own dignity and sanity. You are keeping this part back in case this person isn't 'the one', in case it doesn't work out – so that your dignity can remain intact. This is wise and to be commended – after all, even when a couple are married they are still two separate people; they are not one and the same. They will have their own views, opinions and perspective on life, as discussed in the last chapter.

However, paradoxically, if you keep too much back you might prevent love from ever flowering fully. You can't keep the 'just in case' mentality forever if you are going to be vulnerable and open enough to fall in love. The 'too much' that you have kept back may poison the relationship so that you can't be honest with the other person. It might keep you from really getting to know one another, or worse, be the beginning of the end.

So you do need to open yourself up and put your heart on the line eventually. Now, I'm not talking committing on the first date here, or the second, third or even tenth. There are no rules – it depends entirely on the two people and the pace that they are comfortable with. But I would suggest keeping a good momentum to the first few dates, so that you know for sure you are both interested (and so you don't waste too much time). I would also advocate kicking up a gear after three successful dates – or perhaps a month of dating.

Having given it three dates, you probably need to have a conversation with yourself and ask yourself if this is someone you could have a future with. It sounds intense and serious, and in many ways it is; but it is essential to ask, so that you can be fair on yourself and fair on the other person. If you are looking for 'the one' then casual dating can really only take you so far . . .

Depending on who you are and who the object of your affection is, you may or may not want to discuss this with him or her at this stage. If they are the kind of person who will run away screaming it's probably best not to. If they are the type who wear their heart on their sleeve they may have already said it to you – and you may have run away screaming . . . or not if you like them! If you are the type who might run away screaming, then you might want to admit it to yourself, but tacitly – under your breath, as it were.

I hope you are still with me!

Either way, I think that after three or four dates you will need to address the following question in whatever way suits you best:

'Can I see a future with this person? Do I want to pursue it further?'

In some cases you will know that this person is not the right one for you – in which case you should gently let them go, having caused them the minimum of pain and upset. Whatever you do, don't let it drag on if you can't see potential. Alternatively, you may have struck gold (it does happen!), and you might say 'yes, I can see a future – this could go somewhere'. In which case you can continue and allow the attachment to grow.

In some cases you may not be sure – although I am not entirely convinced about this. I think you frequently know whether or not something is worth pursuing. I do have quite a bit of dating experience now, and I have to say that in all twenty cases I knew whether this was someone I could see a potential future with or not after just two or three dates.

If the answer is an honest 'yes – I can see this going somewhere because I really like the person' (not because I want to be loved or I need someone now, but because I genuinely like them) then congratulations – you are on the right track.

If everybody honestly asked themselves these questions three dates in, when things should still be quite light and non-serious, then there would be a lot more clarity.

Of course, a 'yes' is no guarantee of success or a long and happy future together, but at least you know there is a chance of it, and that you are getting involved with this person for the right reasons – because you genuinely like them and not because you are scared of being alone or just lonely.

The man's prerogative?

This is going to sound incredibly old fashioned to some of you (and even to myself), but I do think that it falls better to the man to give a relationship its momentum in the early stages, and take the initiative. In my experience it just works better. I have attempted to be the one pushing it forwards and it has never worked. End of this bit of the book.

Let go lightly

If you are at that stage of life where you are dating with serious intent of finding your life partner, you need to learn the art of letting something go if it is not working. It can be incredibly painful but it does help that at each stage of putting your heart on the line, you can know that God has everything in hand.

I have attempted to be the one pushing it forwards and it has never worked

Looking back over my past relationships, about seven years ago I went out with a friend and it was one of the best relationships I have ever had. It was in a three-month slot, just before I went away on a voluntary programme in Tanzania. I think it worked so well because I let myself relax, knowing that I was going away and didn't need to worry about the future. I was a very different person then, not looking for something that would last. Now I think of the future much more than I did, which is good in its way. But I did learn an important lesson through that relationship – the importance of simply letting something happen organically. Because I was going away I thought I should make the most of the time with my boyfriend, and enjoy it. I think we all need to do that in our current relationships – not worry so much about the future that we ruin the present.

The next story is a small sketch of some people I observed in a London pub one afternoon while sitting alone, waiting for a bridesmaid dress to be adjusted. I hope it will show how our time on this earth is limited, and we really do need to allow ourselves to go about the business of loving each other now, because one day it will be too late.

A pub in East Croydon

I had been getting a bridesmaid dress fixed in East Croydon and had a few hours to kill before the adjustments were done. It was getting too late for coffee shops to be open, so I headed into a nearby pub.

A lady with a bald head and her friend were sitting next to the only empty table. I nearly trod on their shopping as I sat down. They had a *lot* of shopping – they must have been on a big spree. I noticed that they were getting quite drunk. One empty wine bottle stood on their table and they were onto their next.

Opposite the two ladies sat a man with a long face which was getting longer as the amount of liquid in his pint glass got smaller. The man was watching the two ladies, getting interested in them. I could see he was gearing up to say something. Eventually he leaned over and pointed to his own head while nodding at the bald lady: 'You OK?' he gestured slightly drunkenly towards her head, swaying forward in his chair.

She didn't hear the question as she was deep in conversation with her friend. I could make out some of what she was saying: 'I love my life, I love my husband, my friends, my kids. I just want to live.'

The bald lady smiled back and patted the seat beside her

'Hey!' It was the drunk man again. 'I said – you OK?'

This time she couldn't help but hear him and looked over.

'Yes, I'm OK,' she said in a reserved way. Assessing him, she seemed to make a decision to engage, and continued: 'You don't look very happy though? What's happened in your life?'

He smiled sadly.

The bald lady smiled back and patted the seat beside her. 'Come and sit over here with us. Tell us what's wrong.'

He moved seats immediately and gratefully.

'So – what's up?'

'I split up with my wife. She was sleeping with my brother.'

'Oh,' said the woman.

The man shook his head. 'S'nothing.' He looked again at her head. 'So what's wrong with you?'

'Cancer.'

'How old are you?'

'Forty-two.'

'Well you've had a good run.'

She looked severely unimpressed. 'It's not a good run – forty-two,' she sighed. 'So why are you so upset about your wife – it isn't that big a deal. You should be smiling right now. Your life's really good. What's your name?'

'Bob.'

Bob took her hand and held it for a moment.

'There's still a heart beating in there,' he said, smiling into the eyes of the bald woman as though they were in love.

'Do you smoke?' he asked her.

'I've never smoked a cigarette in my life.'

'They say one in three people has it – it's just in their body,' he mused.

'What's that?' she asked.

'Cancer.'

At this point they started talking more quietly and I couldn't hear what they were saying any more. But I could see they were looking at family photos and cooing over how handsome Bob's sons were. It was like death was hovering over the table, but they were so bravely cheerful and optimistic in the face of it that it didn't seem to have any power at all.

I suddenly thought of a friend of mine whose dad had died of cancer. I had to suppress the urge to text him telling him to eat some green vegetables for supper – spinach or broccoli. A massive fear welled up inside me, then subsided. In that moment I made a promise to myself that wherever I found love I would cherish every minute of it because one day, one way or another, it would come to an end. I made the promise to myself and to God in that moment.

Then it struck me that there was no difference between the bald lady and me – she was just more aware of her death, because it was with her – visible. But it is here with each one of us. As I sat in that pub I thought about talking to her, trying to tell her something about Jesus – but decided it would seem wrong and out of place – or I didn't have the guts . . . you choose. So I prayed inside instead.

Meanwhile the friend buoyed her up with cheery comments, jokes and booze. The bald lady hooted with laughter, bent over her wine glass and the friend did the same. There was a kindness about them, a welcoming spirit. They were genuinely enjoying life and interested in the people around them.

They watched the football together, both commenting in their own ways

It was love between them – the friends.

I wondered what other stories there were in the pub. I looked around.

There was an older man sitting in the corner with his grown-up son, who was in a wheelchair. The man had probably spent the last thirty years caring for his son. He will probably do it until he dies. Father chatted to son, smiling and laughing. They watched the football together, both commenting in their own ways.

It was love between them – the father and son.

Over on the other side of the room some young men were planning a night on the town. As I listened, I realized one of them was in the Army – home on leave, soon to go back again and all too aware that he would not live for ever. The other two were teasing him, nudging him with their elbows, showing their affection and their fear.

It was love between them – these lads.

Love is difficult and complicated. It does not respect time, place or person, but it is one of the best and highest things we can find in the world.

I think it honours God to honour the love we can find in life. So look for it, and seize hold of it when it comes your way, because you don't have very much time.

14

BEING 'GOOD LOOKING'

Fact: In Albania there are thirty different words to describe the shape of eyebrows and forty-five words to describe moustaches

We live in a world that is preoccupied with appearances. In some of the younger, trendier churches looks can become an obsession. Fashion becomes paramount, and everyone is trying to keep up with the latest craze – plastering themselves with make-up, dying their hair until it gets brittle, and slapping on their Christian smiles before the Sunday morning service. Even worse, church can become a place where only the beautiful people are invited to be up on stage talking or leading worship. How does that fit in with Jesus' vision for us?

I think church, as a community of people, should be a place where people are valued for their own unique, individual beauty – not for how closely we can conform to what is paraded across our television screens and down the Hollywood red carpets.

Twenty-one times

Let me tell you about something one of my dates, Simon, and I discussed. This man lives near the seaside, and he loves to eat fish and shellfish – especially oysters. I have only tried oysters once and have to say I hated them. Maybe it was the thought of having to swallow a raw, slug-like thing, all salty and sea-weedy. I'm not a fussy eater at all, but this is the one food that I officially don't like. The one time I tried them, I just about managed to get one down my throat, but felt sick for the rest of the day.

When I told Simon this, he said that it's a well-known fact that if you try something twenty-one times you will grow to like it, even if at first you didn't. He claims to have made himself like olives, anchovies and oysters in this way, and he reckons it can work with anything.

I wonder if you can learn to love anything if you try it twenty-one times. I don't know. But it's got to be worth finding out. Oysters might end up being your favourite food. You've missed out big-time if you don't try. As for me, God has whispered in my ear in that surprising way he has. I have a suspicion that the rule of twenty-one might be as true of dating and wibbly feelings of attraction as it is with oysters. I have a strong feeling that if I was to go on twenty-one dates with a man I found only tolerable-looking at first, and those dates were fun and interesting, I would fancy the pants off him by the end. Sadly, I haven't had the opportunity to test this theory. Maybe one day I will – I hope so.

I would fancy the pants off him by the end

So the first lesson of this chapter is that looks can be deceiving. Sometimes you think someone is utterly gorgeous from a distance, but as soon as you get up close and hear them talk you are completely put off. And it can work the other way round too. You might not be particularly attracted to someone at first, but as you get to know them and find out more about them, their sparkly personality, dazzling wit, compassion, intelligence and sense of humour win you over and you fall in love with their looks later on.

The sticky truth

However, following this analysis, I must do a quick about-turn. We all know the sticky truth that attraction and looks do count. People do decide who they fancy based on whether they are physically attracted to that person. And we all judge people on their looks – without exception! So given this is the case, I am going to put forward the argument for making the most of what you have got.

In practical terms this means looking the best that you can, in your own individual way, and never just slumming it. It could mean that as a girl you might wear a bit of make-up or a skirt from time to time – to whatever level you feel comfortable with. As a guy you might want to buy a new shirt once in a while, or at least choose to wear a clean one.

Also please, sorry to have to say this, but blokes – sort out your smell! In this day and age there is no excuse for being pongy. And no – girls don't find it 'manly', they find it repulsive. If you are from the tribe of men that have not yet discovered deodorant, may I humbly suggest that you get out to Boots, look for the section marked 'masculine hygiene' (or whatever they call it) and get yourself sorted with a bottle of something fragrant!

Of course, in the end, if your personalities clash, no amount of eyeliner or aftershave is going to bring you together. But if you are perfect for each other that little bit of effort at the start to draw you together can make all the difference. Surely you would agree it's better not to be physically repelled by his smell, or to fail to notice her because she is hunched in a huge baggy jumper staying as still as a mouse in the hope that nobody will come up and speak to her ever, ever, ever.

The effect we are hoping for is for the object of your affection to be intrigued by you and want to know more . . . It doesn't mean that you have to be perfect, just be the best that God made you to be.

All shapes and sizes!

A friend of mine recently ran into an ex-girlfriend. Things hadn't worked out between them because they were living a long distance from each other. Well he was amazed and delighted to see her, and astounded by how much she had changed. He said she was as beautiful as ever, but had put on a little weight. Two and a half stones in fact. However, she looked great. Why? Because (according to the guy) the fat had landed in 'all the right places'! The 'right places'? I was amazed. Surely there are

He said she was as beautiful as ever, but had put on a little weight

no 'right places' for fat to land?! But apparently there are. He didn't elaborate on where exactly the right places are but I think I can guess.

Anyway, the point of this story is that you shouldn't assume the person you are hoping to attract is conforming to the stereotypes of what men or women find attractive. There are all sorts of people out there and all sorts of tastes.

A word for those among us who have a shape they are not happy with. I would count myself in this category, as would many people I imagine. Most men are not looking for the Hollywood stereotype. You know the one – stick thin, with no hips and enormous boobs. Most men are actually looking for a real woman – hooray!

It works the other way too; most women are not looking for Mr Muscle. One of my friends has a penchant for the larger man. She likes chunky blokes, verging on chubby – she always has. It so happens that she is not chubby herself – in fact she is slim and shapely. Over the years she has been out with a series of lovely, cuddly men, and I always feel proud of her for going for the guys she really likes and not conforming to the 'good looking' norm – whatever that is.

My point is that God made each one of us quite deliberately to be the way we are, and we should be proud of the way he has made us. So if you're a large-bottomed, big-bosomed lady don't shrink into the corner – be confident with what God gave you, and don't give a hoot what the world thinks. People will respect you for it in the long-term, and you will attract a mate – I guarantee it! You should also know that there are lots of small-boobed women out there (e.g. me) who would love to have what you have, so do us the honour of enjoying what you've got!

And if you are a short, slightly weedy man don't hide your light and think you're not worth it – you totally are.

Someone will come along one day who knows in their heart, body and soul that you are hotter than a hot potato. You give that person a lot better chance of realizing it if you are confident and happy with who you are.

(Oh, and wearing a bit of make-up or changing your underpants every day helps, too, guys and girls.)

Frozen assets?

Everyone has a good asset. Some of us are even lucky enough to have two good assets! So figure out what your best asset is and use it. Because if you are serious about attracting someone worthwhile, you might as well use everything going to make sure that you succeed. Don't always think of the obvious ones – arms can be very attractive, necks, hands, eye, faces, feet.

If your best asset is your face then congratulations! You have struck Christian looks gold! For a start, the face is the bit of you that is on display the most, except perhaps for your hands, and it's quite legitimate to show it off. Secondly, it is the most expressive and communicative part of you – the bit that does all the talking, and most of the connecting with your mate on a day-to-day basis. Even if you have the best sexual connection in the world, you are not going to spend all your time locked together in coital bliss, or even half your time. However, you will spend a lot of your time looking each other in the eye and reading the facial signals. So if you like your face, be encouraged!

However, if you feel a bit ambivalent about your face, or if you actively hate it – don't worry. The chances are that there is something that lights it up from within – something that will appeal to people. And sometimes the most perfect and regular features are not the most

Ever heard of ugly-beautiful? Or even interesting-beautiful?

fascinating or alluring. Ever heard of ugly-beautiful? Or even interesting-beautiful? Being a bit lop-sided can be a plus point, as it keeps life interesting. And the spirit that animates your face from within is far more important! Also, everyone but everyone has beautiful eyes. Fact.

If your best asset is somewhere else then you have a bit more of a problem displaying it to a potential mate, but don't worry – hinting is just as alluring!

Dressing for a date!

I remember when I first found out the meaning of 'high maintenance' and 'low maintenance'. For years I had thought it was something to do with whether a person got easily tired or not. It was quite a revelation when I discovered that it's actually about how much time and effort someone puts into their appearance.

You can probably put yourself somewhere on the maintenance continuum. If like me you are naturally low maintenance, it won't suit you to act high maintenance – you will look fake or forced in your appearance – like you're trying too hard. Don't follow the latest trends for the sake of it – wear things that suit you. Don't slap on foundation and lipstick if you know it makes you look like a clown. If you're naturally high maintenance you will probably feel naked without make-up and unable to go out of the door without straightening your hair. Again, stay with what makes you feel comfortable.

What I'm trying to say is, when you're going out on a first date, don't change how you normally are – just be you. Do make an effort of course – be your own unique version of stylish. But don't try to be something or someone you are not – just think of the effort it will take to continue the illusion! The most important thing you can do is to believe you are attractive. This will come across in how you hold yourself and what you communicate to the other person. The second most important thing you can do is to believe it when someone else tells you that you're beautiful. Not always easy, but you are!

Oh yes, and whatever you decide to wear, never, ever get changed in the loo on trains on the way to your date. It can lead to some very sticky moments involving doors and failure to lock them – I speak from personal experience.

Height restrictions do not apply

A final word: don't get hung up on height. You might miss out on an amazing relationship if you make this a deal-breaker.

A few questions . . .

Where are you on the 'maintenance' continuum?

Are you doing enough to look your version of the best; to be the sparkly, unique, attractive you that you are? Do you wear exactly the same things when you are out and about as you wear when eating fried egg sandwiches at home in front of *The Bill*? If so, then try doing one small thing to make yourself feel a little bit more attractive when you leave the house this week. And if you are not planning on leaving the house, then for goodness' sake, do!

Maybe you are at the other end of the scale? Do you attach too much importance to looks? Are you constantly trying to be the best-turned-out in church, leading your thoughts away from God and other people? If so, then when you catch yourself obsessing over what you look like, try focusing on something else. Keep doing it until it becomes a habit.

Maybe you have got the balance right – you look the best you can without worrying about it too much? Congratulations – you don't need to do anything, except continue reading!

15

SEX

'Daughters of Jerusalem, I charge you by the gazelles and by the does of the field: Do not arouse or awaken love until it so desires'
– Song of Songs 2:7

I met him at a Christian singles Christmas party. He was jaw-droppingly good-looking. Tall, dark-haired, tanned, dressed in black. He was a dancer, a smooth salsa man. He worked his way around the room – getting into all the ladies' personal spaces. But he wasn't drunk – he was just in love with dancing.

I was there with my friend Emma. That festive season had been spent going to lots of Christian singles parties like this, and we were becoming experts at the format.

We danced to a few cheesy, Christmassy numbers; enjoying the free-styling awkwardness of most people there. Then completely unexpectedly the sexy dancer-man schmoozed up to us on the dance floor. I think maybe I got too relaxed with my dancing and unintentionally attracted him somehow. I immediately seized up and couldn't move my legs or arms in time to the music. He was unperturbed by this, and grabbed my hands. He tried to teach me to salsa, his slim mobile hips far too close for comfort! I didn't know how to react. I can't dance at all, let alone in the proximity of a ridiculously attractive man. I tried a few little spins. I got dizzy. I am not sure if the dizziness was because of the spinning or the man.

Anyway, Emma and I mutually decided that it was time to go. I was slightly relieved to be escaping the man's dance-floor attentions, but we did swap phone numbers before I went.

His name was 'a.k.a Milos' according to what he wrote on the scrap of paper he gave me. He looked bored when I tried to engage him in conversation. That was all I knew at this stage. We arranged by text message to meet the following weekend.

The trophy boyfriend?

Before I met up again with Milos, my housemate Atheist Andy teased me plenty, because I unfortunately told Andy about Milos' stunning looks. Andy said I should change the title of this book to *How to Get a Trophy Boyfriend or Handsome Christian Hunks – How to Find Your Very Own.*

I was very nervous before this date. Pre-date nerves seem to be part of the package when you are out on the dating scene. The other side of this is that you are never bored I suppose. As soon as the nerves disappear, it's probably time to take a break from dating.

Pre-date nerves seem to be part of the package when you are out on the dating scene

Milos and I had arranged to meet at Piccadilly Circus, just outside Boots. I got there early so loitered around the lip balm. Like many women my age I have an addiction to lip balm which started at school. A confident voice interrupted my thoughts about whether flavoured or plain lip balm was better: 'Hello.'

I looked up from the Chapsticks, and there he stood. Yes – this was how I remembered him. Dark-haired, impossibly good looking, husky voiced. I smiled in a flustered, shy way. He smiled back and we headed out into the London night.

The bar he took me to was big and intimidating. Everything was black and red. Sleek black bar surfaces, shiny red chairs, modern art dotted around, clouds of perfume and expensive aftershave that we walked through. The clientele were sleek London-city types in black, white and grey with impossibly tall heels, suits and impossibly neat hair. I felt like a country bumpkin in my blue top.

'Let me show you around. It's a good place,' he said, sounding like he owned it.

He steered me up the stairs with his arm. My mind thought, 'Wrong! No steering. Especially not on a first date. Probably not ever – I'm not a car or a horse.' And yet, something about it felt good.

'I don't belong here,' I thought as I waited for my drink, keeping my cardigan wrapped tightly round me and trying to disappear into the background.

'I really don't go with this man,' I thought as I followed him through the crowd. 'I mean – look at this place. This is mad. Look at him . . .' I looked at Milos' back view . . .

We found a table, sat down and chatted for a bit, but not much. I tried to engage him in conversation about a giant tiger made of metal coat-hangers which was stuck to the ceiling. But he didn't seem interested and pretty soon he wanted to get dancing – of course – true to form.

He must have kissed a lot of girls to have lip balm knowledge like that!

As he swung me around the dance floor, I felt my head starting to go – reason leaving and the law of the rhythm of the music and wine taking over. It didn't matter that this man and I had barely anything in common I decided. This felt good, so it was good.

I felt like maybe I did belong here after all. Maybe I was this really sexy, attractive woman who could dance. Maybe I was as gorgeous as he kept saying I was . . .

Then suddenly, we were kissing.

I do love kissing, and Milos was a great kisser. He knew what he was doing. At one point he pulled away from the kiss and looked into the distance with a thoughtful expression, rubbing his lips together as if wine tasting.

'Boots own brand vanilla rescue lip balm,' he said with a quick wolfish smile, eyebrows lifting away from glittering eyes.

I was startled. He must have kissed a lot of girls to have lip balm knowledge like that! But I shrugged inwardly, smiled and leant in for another kiss.

So Milos and I continued dancing, sipping our wine and kissing.

I was misbehaving, I admit. But I'm generally a good girl and the next thing that happened surprised me a lot.

Milos moved in closer as we danced and whispered something in my ear. I couldn't hear because the music was so loud.

'What?' I yelled.

'I said – shall we go to my car?' he yelled back, ultra-loud.

I couldn't quite believe what I had heard. But I had heard right.

'Shall we go to my car?'

'Are you joking?'

I pulled away from him in shock. He had driven into central London? Driven? No-one drives into central London. But he had. I could only conclude that this was some sort of pre-meditated plan to get me in the back of his car. On a first date. And I had a feeling it wasn't the first time he had done this. Then I shivered and looked at him as if seeing him for the first time. A strange chill went through me.

'Why are you looking like that? I just asked . . .'

'Who *are* you?' I said to him, taking his hands off my waist.

'Hey – what are you getting so excited about? Calm down.' He reached for my glass. 'Here, just have a drink.'

'No, wait a minute – who, what, who exactly are you?'

'I'm . . . Milos.'

The moment passed. He was just a beautiful, sad man. The shadow that had passed across his face and through me was gone.

'Hmm . . . nothing.' I shook my head.

'So you don't want to . . .'

'No – I do *not* want to go to your car.'

What interests me, looking back, is that this man is a fully-fledged member of a very large and well-known church in London that he has been attending for a long time. And yet, he thinks a request for casual sex (or some serious fooling around at least) on the first date is absolutely fine.

After I refused to go to his car, he told me I was a good lady – a real Christian. I didn't feel like a good Christian as I was still thinking about the kiss. He changed a bit after this and was a lot more respectful for the rest of the evening. Still, there was no way I would be going on a second date with him if he suggested it. He never did.

So what did I learn from this experience? It doesn't take a genius to guess. Are you sitting comfortably? Because I've got some news for you – news that is true . . .

Super-date discovery

Chemistry and sexual attraction are not what it is all about!

They really, genuinely aren't! They are important, but the 'tingly feeling' is just the icing on the cake of friendship, laughter, mutual respect, shared interests and all the other zillions of fascinating ingredients that go into making a good relationship. So hold onto your hypothalamuses and please don't get carried away by physical attraction. You can't build love on it.

Now, I've always known that this was true, but I haven't really felt it deep down. And I certainly haven't always acted as if it's true. I have frequently got on board the emotionally empty train of falling for someone because of physical attraction. More often than not this falling has all taken place in my own head – daydreams, night-dreams, distraction at work. Imagination is a powerful thing. It can take over and build phantoms that draw you away from God and real life. Before long you wake up and wonder where the time went. Even if you never act on it, sexual infatuation can make you waste the time that God has given you, or make you point your energy and drive in the wrong direction.

I hope that Milos was my end paper to that sort of nonsense.

In my eyes, he was a physically perfect man – a fantastic kisser, very attractive, but *completely* lacking in any of the right features in other respects. At no point was I getting in that car with him. And I really learnt the lesson this time. It couldn't be clearer.

We do all feel the urge to have sex, we are human after all

We do all feel the urge to have sex, we are human after all. It's how we deal with that urge that counts, and the ability to recognize it for what it is – not the pang of true love but of something a lot more basic. Sometimes it comes in the guise of beauty – a little lust to dispel the day-to-day drudgery, a little warmth to burn off the loneliness. These things can quickly control us if we are not careful.

Know your enemy, as they say. It's a good start.

It was interesting to compare Milos with some of my other dates.

There were no physical fireworks on several of my favourite dates. No kisses or even a hint that a kiss might happen. No holding hands. No wibbly feeling in the stomach. But since I started writing this book I've been on a journey and I'm no longer sure that wibbly feelings are as important as I thought. The wibbly feeling is a fickle thing. It can be there intensely strongly at a first meeting then quickly fade when you find out what the person is actually like. It also has a tendency to appear when the other person is unavailable, taken or married, which is very revealing. This suggests that the wibbly feeling can be easily manipulated by the darker forces in the world, something that we really need to watch out for.

A question for you

Is it more important that you are intensely physically attracted to the person you marry, or that they are your best friend and confidant?

PART III

READY

In which some things are examined that can give you the strength, emotional steadiness and self-belief to embark on your quest for a partner. In which I also look at the unexpected places that love can appear.

16

HAPPINESS

The question: What is one of the most important things that parents can teach their children?
The answer: To love themselves and be happy.

One day I was chatting with a friend of mine. We were talking about moodiness and happiness. I asked if he got dark moods ever and he said, 'I like to be happy.'

'What a weird thing to say,' I replied, 'of course you like to be happy; I like to be happy too – it doesn't mean that I always am, or that I can somehow induce happiness.'

And he just smiled (we were on the phone at the time, but I could tell he was smiling).

My friend's words that day stayed with me. What puzzled me was the way that he said it – as though happiness was not dependant on external circumstances at all, but was something that could be built up or summoned up at will.

Then I thought about it some more and I realized my friend was right. Happiness is in many ways a habit and a choice. It is built up in the small gestures and the ways that you deal with things on a day-to-day basis, until it becomes so seamless that it becomes part of your personality – part of the way you react to the world. There is no secret key to happiness, or magic to it – most people can simply learn it. I exclude from this some depressives who might have an imbalance of chemicals in their brain, but for most of us happiness actually is a choice.

There is no secret key to happiness, or magic to it – most people can simply learn it

A few weeks later I saw a programme on TV that seemed to confirm this. It was about the synapses in our brain and it used computer animation to bring the brain alive. It was one of those programmes where you are half way through watching and you realize that you are leaning forward in awe with your mouth hanging open, just simply astounded at what you are seeing. The narrator described how your personality is formed, and showed the surface of someone's brain looking like a landscape in a storm being struck by lightning. The lightning was a visual representation of a synapse firing and hitting a receptor to create a thought. Different thoughts hit different areas of the brain and the voiceover told me that if we have similar thought responses a lot of the time, the brain will learn that pattern and start to do it automatically.

What does all this have to do with dating? Well, if we can train our brains and unlearn thought patterns, we can also unlearn negative dating patterns. I thought of the lightning theology then, and the way we can shape our own destinies, because God has given us choice. I thought of the power and beauty in that – and the responsibility. Maybe some would question the idea of a

Christian thinking of herself as a self-made creation, but I believe God gave us brains and choice for a reason.

Knowing that we make our own personalities through learned responses could mean unlearning the toxic patterns that stop us from being good dates or spouses . . . and many other even more important things like overcoming anger or mild depression. Which leads me neatly on to Lawrence.

Lawrence – wisteria and hysteria

Lawrence went against my usual dating rules because he went to my church. Still, if I've learnt one thing while looking for a partner, it's that there are always exceptions to the rules! We both arrived for the morning service at the same time, walking, four weeks in a row. He looked vaguely familiar to me with his round face, tousled dark hair and green eyes. On the fourth occasion I decided to talk to him. After a bit of chatting we realized that we had met years ago through a mutual friend. At that time he had long bleached-blonde hair and an ambition to be a novelist. I had the same ambition (without the bleached-blonde hair) and we had a good chat about it. Neither of us were Christians back then.

These were all very strange God-incidences, I thought, and it led me to get quite interested in Lawrence.

Lawrence was a strange one: very quiet, shy and nervous, but also sensitive, funny, caring and imaginative. He was a great deal more than he believed he was.

It turned out that Lawrence lived in a house right opposite mine. It was a house I had often looked at with pleasure, because it was covered with beautiful blossoming purple wisteria. Lawrence lodged with an old man he called 'Grandpa'. He worried about 'Grandpa' a lot and tried to get him to go out of the house from time to time to meet friends. You could see Lawrence's bedroom window from my own. He was literally the boy-next-door. I visited his house once and it was full of poetry books, bits of artwork and eccentric items from a bygone era. I loved it.

He played guitar to me hesitantly . . . and sang softly and dolefully.

Lawrence had a spluttering old car which was all eaten away by rust. You could see the road through the bottom of the bodywork in one place. The tarmac rushed past just a few inches away from our feet. Lawrence was an extremely nervous driver but he laughed at himself while we tried to drive around Watford together, parking a million miles from where we were meant to be because it was easier.

Funny things happened when Lawrence was around. Everything seemed brighter and more interesting. We went to see some local musicians at an open-mike night. Lawrence's friend Mitch came with us. Mitch has learning difficulties and Lawrence said he liked to hang out with him because Mitch made him happy – and I could see why. Mitch was hilarious. He compèred the open-mike night, which was a motley array. There was a lady who sang the Kate Bush song 'Washing Machine' in a crazy style. There was a wild-eyed young man with a beautiful wife and baby who sang Western music with his band. There was a

I won a strange musical box with two dancing puppets – male and female

Rasta with long dreadlocks who played delicate classical guitar music to an amazing standard.

There was even a raffle half way through with bizarre unwanted items as the prizes. I won a strange musical box, with two dancing puppets – male and female – controlled by a crazy puppet master in a top hat.

It was all wonderfully eccentric and I would never have known about it if Lawrence had not taken me there.

After we had met up a few times we decided we were going out. It was exciting and hopeful. He said 'let's write poems about how we feel about it'. I laughed at his intensity, and loved it at the same time. 'I'm glad I've found you,' he said with a smile, decisively putting his arm around me, and smiling into my face. It felt so good – like he had claimed me with that action. Something sure and unwavering. We held hands.

Unfortunately we never moved on to kissing, because after three days he phoned me in the middle of the night and said he couldn't go out with me. He was panicking. It was all too much. Then after five days he phoned me at work and said he didn't want to live without me, and could we try after all. Then after seven days he phoned me and said he couldn't do this after all.

I was not very polite to him then.

It turns out that Lawrence was a depressive with various anxiety complexes. I guess it's hard to know what God is saying when you're struggling with those kinds of issues. All I was hearing from God about Lawrence was 'Spend more time together'. I don't think Lawrence could hear what God was saying at all as he was so caught up in his own anxiety and depression.

I put him out of mind a long time ago, and threw away the musical box with the puppets and the puppet master. But writing this has made me feel a bit wistful again. Lawrence will always be one that could have been good. But he just didn't love himself enough.

You deserve to be loved and love in return

You may not have the same issues that Lawrence had, but there is one thing that a lot of us still have to learn – we all deserve love.

You deserve to be loved and love in return.

Fully and wholeheartedly.

Respectfully and passionately.

With laughter and with hope.

You deserve love.

Three little words, but so essential to remember as you fight your way through the dating jungle. Maybe when things are going right it's easy to believe you deserve it. You are feeling confident, sassy and attractive. Or you've just met a new special someone, and are in that starry-eyed zone of getting to know them – the evening phone calls, the text messages during the day and so on. But then he or she dumps you – the rollercoaster crashes, and suddenly there you are again, with the voices in your head . . .

'There must be something wrong with me because I wasn't good enough for them to love me. Maybe this isn't what God has planned for me after all. Maybe I should quit looking.'

I imagine it must be infinitely harder to get over this when it's been a very long relationship – maybe you were engaged or even married. But you absolutely must recover your self-worth after a knock-down or break-up. You owe it to yourself, and you owe it to God. Look at how much he loves you and how he views you. Your price – your unique and wonderful price tag is beyond measure – only God knows how precious you are. He will redeem all your yesterdays and that includes the duff dates and the broken-hearted moments. If it's true that God loves you infinitely, and you can accept God's perfect and baffling love for you, how much easier is it to accept that a human being somewhere will dig you!

Think about how you would react if another person came moping to you saying that they are unlovable

Think about how you would react if another person – one of your friends or family – came moping to you saying that they are unlovable. You wouldn't believe it for a moment. So why is there one rule for them and another for you?

Maybe you are one of those people who has to work at the whole 'liking yourself' thing. If you're the sort of person who has difficulty seeing yourself through rose-tinted spectacles, the sort of person who can't accept a compliment when one comes your way, the sort of person who will hide bchind your fringe and mumble inaudibly if someone says you are pretty or clever, then I have one thing to say to you – stop it! Stop it right now!

Do you think you are doing yourself any favours by being that way – by constantly putting yourself down? Do you think that you are doing your potential (or actual) spouse any favours by diminishing your value? No way! If that special person is worth anything, they will want you to shine like the star that you are, and you can only do that when you are brimming with glorious self-esteem. And you know what will attract them? The confidence of knowing that you are a lovely and shiny imperfect person – just like them.

Imagine this. You go on a date with a complete stunner who has an exciting job, a great personality, can make you laugh and ticks all the other boxes that you have lined up for him or her – let's say him for the sake of argument. However, he spends the whole evening putting himself down, saying things like 'Well, I guess I'm doing OK, but well – I haven't got very far on getting that promotion and I did give up learning the cello when I was fifteen at grade seven, and I never did manage to write that bestseller, and I've never been to Turkey and I guess it's too late now . . .' And so on. You wouldn't be too impressed would you? You would probably walk away from the date feeling quite low and gloomy, thinking 'what was that all about?'

Don't give yourself a 'could-do-better' persona on a first date. Think about how what you say will come across – what if you were sitting opposite yourself at the dinner table? Would you be entertained and delighted by Mr or Ms Sparkly, or would you be tying napkins together to make a rope to hang yourself?

One way to be the best you can on a date is to do something or go somewhere that makes you sparkle and shine. If that's the local park, then go there. If it's the ice-skating rink or a bird hide – go there. Show who you really are through the choice of what you decide to do on your date. (See chapter 8 for some unusual and novel dating ideas.)

Kill the little person in your head

So instead of playing yourself down, why not try a different approach? Try believing that you are an extremely worthwhile prize for anybody and acting like it – not acting like you know it as this might come across as bigheaded – rather, acting like you feel it deep down. If you hear the little voice inside saying 'you know you're not a great prize – you're a booby prize at best, and not even a booby prize because your boobs are much too small . . .' (or whatever particular thing makes you feel most insecure) then kill the little person who is saying it to you, or at least lock him in a box until the date is over.

If necessary keep him under lock and key as you enter a new relationship or as you get to know somebody. Eventually it should get easier and you can start to leave the door unlocked – or even let your little gremlin out altogether so he can leave and take up residence somewhere else. Take as long as you need. When you are loved and love back your insecurities and uncertainties will diminish in that person's company and may even vanish.

In the external world, it could help to avoid situations and people that make you feel down about yourself, or low. You know what those situations are because they zap your energy and make you feel drained. Head for the places and people that lift you up, and make you feel sunny inside.

When your self-esteem is top-notch you carry yourself better, you come across as a good thing, and you attract good things. Now enjoy the good things and get on with finding someone.

Action! Try this:

Write down ten things about yourself that make you smile – then when you are feeling low in self-confidence take a look at the list!

Try keeping a happiness book where you write all the things that are good in the world – or that seem best to you. Things like chocolate, hugs, the sea, snails and tambourines (or whatever floats your boat). Include some of the things that you like about yourself and some of the things you like to do with your friends or family. When you feel rotten about the world sit and read it.

Please believe you are capable of anything. Believe you deserve love. Believe you are beloved already. These are what will do you the most good.

17

HAVING A LIFE AND KEEPING IT!

'Believe that life is worth living and your belief will help create the fact'
– William James

It is a truth universally acknowledged that if you are busy in life, people will come knocking at your door to ask if you might be able to help out with just one more thing . . . If you are not busy and have hours of free time with nothing to do, no-one will come knocking, you will vegetate and grow lonely and fat . . . Well, I'm not sure about the fat part, but in general it is true.

Have you ever noticed that the same thing happens with relationships?

If you are incredibly busy, with barely enough time to do the things you are doing already, very often you will meet someone. Then you have to fit them in somehow – shoehorn them into your overcrowded life.

The strange thing is that the chances are they will respect you for this. They will be intrigued by how committed you are to all these different things – friends, family, music, ballet dancing, whatever is keeping you busy.

This fact has led some people to believe that the best way to win over a man or woman is to pretend to be

All you will be able to do is to create a small raspberry noise

extremely busy and create some imaginary prior appointments and reasons why you can't meet up with them immediately.

Of course, this will inevitably backfire because you are technically lying. One day your beloved will discover that you do not play the tuba, or go scuba-diving at the weekends, or take your tuba scuba-diving, or whatever other impressive hobby you have made up. One day they will ask you to play that tuba or demonstrate good diving technique; and all you will be able to do is to create a small raspberry noise (if you are fortunate enough to actually own a tuba), or sink helplessly to the bottom of the swimming pool and flail about a bit. You could create a ridiculously complex back story about how you had to stop playing the tuba because sadly your instrument became irrevocably water-logged and had to be recycled to make aluminium cans. But no-one would believe that. And who wants to go out with a liar?

So what is the answer?

Well, it's quite simple. If you want to intrigue them with your busy life and your exotic hobbies then guess what? You have to go out there and get a busy life and some exotic hobbies! Start a band, learn Spanish, visit your folks, run a book group, or just run. Volunteer for a local charity, start dance classes, collect stamps. Just do something, anything.

If you want a frivolous reason to get a hobby (apart from the obvious fact you might enjoy it) – it will give you something to talk about on your dates.

If you want a serious reason, I have one of those for you too. From a Christian perspective, keeping busy and not frittering time away is about using your life for God, whether you are single or coupled up – living life to the fullest and enjoying the season you are in. If you are single, at times it may seem like forever, not a season, but once your time of singleness is over there will probably be certain things that you miss about it – the freedom, the self-awareness, the enjoyment of your own company . . . You can eat what you want, go where you like, listen to the music you enjoy, decide when you want to leave the party, decide which parties you want to go to without having to consult or be coerced . . .

But before I talk myself out of a job here – most of us do want a committed, lifelong relationship deep down, even with all the compromises it will inevitably bring. I know I do. I want someone to share life and have new adventures with. And it's OK to admit that to yourself and go for it, whilst pursuing all the other facets of your life.

One other point to note is that unless you start enjoying the present right now, you will become a PSPD – a Person in a State of Perpetual Dissatisfaction. For the PSPD, nothing is quite right, nothing is satisfactory. They are always waiting for the next 'thing', and none of the 'things' quite lives up to their expectations. For a PSPD, marriage, when it does come along, is just another 'thing' that fails to live up to expectations and then turns into something underwhelming that must be sat through like a bad play. Be very wary of perfectionism in seeking your life partner . . .

A final point on busy-ness . . . Don't be busy as a tactic to meet someone, but be busy as a tactic to **be** someone. One of the most enjoyable dating experiences I had was with a man who did lots of things. He was permanently busy and tied up in all manner of projects – full of ideas and fun. He was also one of only two in the twenty that had real potential.

Simon – a man with a life

Simon was introduced to me by his mother. I am not sure whether this is a good thing or not. Anyway, I walked into the kitchen at my uncle's church and found my auntie and Simon's mum chuckling away. And then I was accosted: 'My son's single – you should meet up with him!' Just like that. I found it a little odd that I had met his mum before I met Simon himself. But it was also reassuring in a way. So Facebook was the way forward then.

I was accosted: 'My son's single – you should meet up with him!'

On Facebook Simon seemed lovely. We struck up a bit of a messaging conversation and he seemed really sweet. He asked lots of endearing questions, such as 'what is your favourite childhood toy?' and 'what is your favourite cake?' Simon was not my usual type – more of a rugby player than a football player – but one of the lovely things about this whole process was that I was being challenged to step outside my usual 'type' and go out with people I might not have otherwise considered. This was because one of my ground rules was that I must not turn down the opportunity of a date with anyone. The idea was that, even if things went badly, at least I would have given him a chance and it would only be one evening wasted. In making this rule I have had some great experiences and learnt a lot. I think it is a good rule and I hope you will try it too.

So, through the power of the Book of Faces, our friendship began. I learnt that he once applied for a marketing job at the charity I work at. On Facebook I also discovered that he is a member of the Tea Appreciation Society, he likes Nooma (Rob Bell's books and materials), and he enjoys *Flight of the Conchords* which I also find hilarious. I could almost forgive him for having Top Gear in there too . . . almost . . . So things seemed promising enough for a meet-up to be arranged . . .

A day full of good things

We met in London two weeks before Christmas. It was a weekend of intense flooding throughout England. It absolutely poured that day.

The rendezvous was Trafalgar Square, just outside the National Gallery. The last ten minutes on the Underground I was feeling decidedly sick. Pre-first-date nerves are inevitable I'm afraid. There's just no avoiding them. The other side of this is that it can be a real adrenalin rush – entering the unknown. I was a bit early so I went to the loo (for longer than strictly necessary) and hovered around a bit. Then there he was – looking cheerful and hearty, wearing a pair of specs, a woolly hat and a broad grin.

The rain poured down. It absolutely bucketed. Simon and I walked through deep puddles to Covent Garden, which was alive with Christmas, its spirit not dampened by the rain. Cheerful charity volunteers rattled buckets for Shelter, street entertainers teetered on unicycles, vendors thrust bags of hot roasted chestnuts under our noses, and the soggy people of London put on a brave show of Christmas cheer, decked out in damp scarves and wringing-wet bobble hats.

'How are your feet?' he asked.

'Squelchy,' I replied.

So, to dry out, we headed down to the lower market and into a cosy grotto-like coffee shop. We drank cappuccinos and discovered that we have lots in common – singing, real ale, chocolate factories . . .

Outside again, we saw a man cooking paella in the biggest frying pan I have ever seen. People were queuing up for it hungrily. We bought pie and mashed potato for lunch, served in cardboard boxes, and followed it with rainbow-coloured cupcakes from a pastel-bright cake shop. We ate our lunchtime feast sitting in the downstairs courtyard, and watching the entertainment.

First up was a small opera-singing man with red face and theatrical gestures. Then there was a wonderful string-quintet with added flute who performed in the most vital and energetic way. They flew at the music, using their instruments like dance-props, leaping, bobbing, and can-canning as they played. Any attractive young lady walking past got latched onto and followed around the courtyard by the lead violinist. If an older gentleman looked disinterested they would play pointedly at him until he acknowledged their presence. They gathered around babies and small children who reacted in a variety of ways – from delight to terror. One little girl of about four sat in splendour in her pushchair as the whole outfit crouched down and played directly at her. The look on her face suggested that having her own private orchestra was a daily occurrence for her, and just to be expected!

We emerged out of the Tube onto an Oxford Street which was swimming with water. They had some rather tasteful pale blue-white decorations strung up all along the road and these were reflected in the puddles and off people's damp faces, making the whole street seem alive with liquid silver. After wandering about for a bit and exploring the packed shops, we headed off home, me carrying the box of leftover cupcakes over my head as a makeshift umbrella.

He wants to look at everything, he laughs at everything, he is enthused and excited by everything

I had been having a pretty stressful time at work, with no time to think about Christmas at all. The day I spent in London with Simon felt like the real beginning of the festive season, not least because Simon himself is festivity in the form of a man. Like the ghost of Christmas present in Charles Dickens' *A Christmas Carol*, he is so jolly and good and kind, with his broad, happy smile. He wants to look at everything, he laughs at everything, he is enthused and excited by everything. It's great.

An aside

Things went well with Simon for a bit; but then things went rather quiet, which I was sad about for a while. As it turned out, he had a bit too much of a life at the time I met him. His work was causing him immense stress – he had to work sixteen-hour days a lot of the time, and was flying overseas a lot. Because he lived a long way away as well, the communication just petered out. I understand that communication also stopped with his family and most of his friends at that time, so it wasn't just me.

From this experience I must temper the advice I have given about having a life by saying that yes, it is important to have a life, but it is also important to know what is important.

To unpack that cryptic point: if you are going to have a relationship that works you are going to need to start prioritizing it over a period of time. If you don't you will either have a relationship that is starved of the time and attention it needs and a burden to you both because of it, or you will have no relationship at all.

Finding the right balance is not easy; and of course it helps if you are in the same city as each other; or even nearby cities. An attachment carried out over a long distance needs even more careful nurturing and communication. So maybe find yourself a chatterbox if you are planning to do the distance thing!

Have a think . . .

What things do you do that make you feel alive and yourself? That is, if you stopped doing them you would feel incomplete – like only half the best self you can be. Mine are singing, writing, being outdoors, learning and hugging. Try writing yours down.

If you can't think of any, or your life is empty of any hobbies, interests or passions – change it! Take up a new hobby, volunteer at a local charity, join a church team. Whatever you do, do something – so that when a potential person does arrive in your life they will see that you are a very interesting person with a full life and lots going on. You never know, you could even meet someone through your new hobby.

Then you just need to solve the problem of how to fit that special person into your amazing, busy, balanced life!

18

THE SEVEN STANDARDS

'When people do not respect us we are sharply offended; yet in his private heart no man much respects himself'
– Mark Twain

One of the most distressing things to be told as a single Christian is that you are 'too fussy'. I have been told it frequently. There seems to be a perception that we Christians are looking for perfection. The belief is that all women in the church want someone tall, dark, handsome, witty, well-paid, fond of cooking, sensitive but strong at the same time. I would like to declare right now that this is not true. It is rubbish. Although I suppose if he did happen to come along I wouldn't turn him away.

I decided to try an experiment. I would make a list of just seven 'must-haves' for my partner

I suspect this belief might come from the fact that there are fewer men than women in the church, so of course it looks like we are fussy because there is a smaller pool to choose from.

Having said this, through conversations with various friends I've come to realize that we do all need some standards. You can't really go out and find the right partner for you unless you know what you are looking for.

So I decided to try an experiment. I would make a list of just seven 'must-haves' for my partner – seven 'deal-breakers' that cannot be compromised on – particular to me alone. The only rule was that I had to be strict on only having seven standards. So here they are, my seven deal breakers:

1. Preferably a Christian – if he doesn't share my faith it is going to cause problems, and it's such a big part of who I am and my attitude to life that it makes sense for it to be shared with my partner.
2. About the right age. In my case between 27 and 39. Someone once told me that you can go out with someone half your age plus seven – which means that I could go down to 21, but I think that's pushing it a bit!
3. Would like to have a family one day. I know I want one and there simply wouldn't be a future in it if he doesn't think the same.
4. Similar sense of humour.
5. Kind – this is *so* important and underrated.
6. Intelligent – doesn't have to be a genius, just about the same as me, or a bit above to challenge me and make me think.
7. Attractive to me – doesn't have to be stunning by the world's standards, but must appeal to me.

I didn't find it easy to make this list.

There are things that I would have loved to put in but are really optional extras. Things like curiosity, enthusiasm, a passion for learning and reading, enjoying travel and music, a sense of justice, getting on well with my family . . . Being taller than me and having dark hair were also in my 'long-list'. I could go on.

But, so as not to be fussy, only seven are allowed, so the list was duly whittled down. By restricting the list to seven essentials and agreeing to be open-minded about everything else, I've realized what really matters and what might make me (and God!) happiest.

So here's an invitation for you. Go and make your own list now. Go and write down the seven things that you must have in a soul mate. Do it prayerfully, and thoughtfully. Maybe discuss it with a friend to see what he or she thinks.

Of course your list will be different to mine – chemistry might be more important to you (the attraction kind, not the school subject kind), good communication or certain interests such as travel or skydiving might be hugely important to you. The only thing that matters is that you limit your list to seven, and *only* seven items.

Then when you've made your list and you're happy with it, try sticking to it!

It might feel a little weird at first. It might feel a little cold and calculating to judge potential partners by these seven standards, but it will probably save you a lot of heartache if you do because it might stop you from making some of the mistakes you are now making. Mistakes like chasing people because of their looks, or skidding into unfortunate relationships because someone shows a vague interest. It may even stop you from marrying someone who seems ideal for a while, but who will make you miserable in the long-term.

All I know is that making my list of seven Godly standards has helped me to get real about who I'm looking for. What I found was that when I started to employ the list, strange things started to happen. I began to look at people in a different light, and suddenly everything was turned around. Since I made my list and started sticking to it, my heart has been mended and changed in so many ways.

So, say you make your list and employ it. You might finally get to talk to that gorgeous worship leader who your heart has been fluttering over for weeks; but instead of thinking 'He's so cool and gorgeous' you think 'Does he have a sense of humour about himself?' Or maybe when the girl with the cute dimples and blonde hair is flirting with you, instead of thinking 'I love the way she laughs like that with her head tipped back', you think 'Would we actually have things to talk about with each other every day for the rest of our lives?'

The answer is often 'no'.

It is reality hitting.

But it is a good kind of reality, because it knocks the fantasy on the head. It kills it stone dead.

Why is that good? Because it unlocks the door for the person who is going to enrich your life and bring you closer to God in so many ways.

Finally you can recognize a man who will make you smile and feel like a real prize of great price. Finally you can clearly see a woman who will love you all her life, making you laugh and brightening each day that you spend together.

Finally you can recognize a man who will make you smile and feel like a real prize of great price

The people who match up to your seven standards may not be the popular or beautiful ones, but they can be just perfect for you – and you for them. You might experience the same thing I did and start to look at potential partners in a very different way. It might be quite beautiful. You might find love in an unexpected place.

Of course, if your list of requirements says things like 'must be gorgeous; charming; popular; must have a good body; a wonderful way with words' you might find it a little difficult to achieve all seven, and your fish may escape.

However, if you also put 'must be loyal' and 'crazy about me' in there too you'll be OK! Just listen to your heart and pray as you write your list and God will do the rest.

And by the way – if you put the same number 7 as me – attractive, or a version of it – don't dismiss someone if they match up in every other way. Attraction is a fickle thing (especially for us women); – it can come and go, grow and wane. So don't attach too much importance to them having a certain look. That's why I left 'dark hair' off the list but kept in 'attractive to me', which is about as open as you can be while still admitting that looks count.

Once you've found the person God wants you to be with, I'm sure you're going to feel there is such a feast of subtlety and richness waiting for you that you will wonder what you ever saw in your fantasy figure.

Lecture over – give it a try. It's fun apart from anything else!

Action!

Make your list of seven standards and stick to it!

19

FRIENDSHIP

'I know you of old'
– Beatrice to Benedict, Much Ado About Nothing,
William Shakespeare

As you go on your own dating journey, it's hugely important to pursue close friendships with members of the opposite sex so that you realize they are not alien beings – and that we have a lot in common. Also to know that not all opposite-sex relationships mean that you are going to fancy them or get romantically involved.

One of my best male friends is Atheist Andy, who I have mentioned briefly earlier in this book. Andy has been my friend and housemate throughout the whole process of my documented search for a guy – from the initial idea, through the research stage to the end product. He has been a sounding board, an observer, a shoulder to cry on and an irritation in equal measure.

Before you start speculating (as I know I would in your position, you naughty gossiping people!), I just want to clarify that Andy is simply a friend. Firstly, he doesn't fulfil at least two of my seven standards, and these really are essential in my long-term partner. Secondly, ever since I met him he has belonged to our mutual friend Helen – secretly at first, and openly now. Until recently Helen had not quite realized that she liked him back, but fortunately she now has. They are going out, and everything is as it should be – and indeed always has been.

If you are thinking of setting up a profile on a dating website, I would strongly recommend that you get a friend to write your profile

Anyway, he is a great friend. Having said this I must say that I have decided not to follow most of Andy's advice; especially his suggestion that I change the title of the book to *The Musings of Atheist Andy and His Sidekick Christian Flatmate*. I think not. However, he has been very useful in other ways. For example, he helped to write my profile for a couple of dating sites. If you are thinking of setting up a profile on a dating website, I would strongly recommend that you get a friend to write your profile. They can see you better than you can see yourself and may be bolder at articulating your good points.

Of course, Andy and I have our differences – not least the take on faith. Some Friday evenings see us sitting with our Bibles, reading sections to each other. (Yes, we are that cool.) He chooses really 'fire and brimstone' type passages from the Old Testament while I read friendly passages from the New; each of us trying to prove points about the nature of God. One evening I read 1 Corinthians 13; he had never heard it before – he doesn't go to many Christian weddings! He liked it – he didn't admit as much, but I could tell because he went quiet, and he let it rest as the last passage in that particular battle. And it did trump his reading of Exodus 21 verse 7.

And boy, have I learnt a lot about boys over the last year of living with him. He spent the whole of one month farting, talking about farts and texting about farts. And then it ended, as suddenly as it began. He is so uncomplicated and wants a quiet life really. He mocks constantly. He knows how to make gadgets work and how to fix things and the rules of cricket. He doesn't do the washing up until the pile has reached alarming proportions and there are no more cups for tea. Of course, not all boys/men are like this – but I think there are a few recurring patterns!

A question of friendship

In the car one day, my old housemate Anna and I were chatting about dating and our male friends. She suggested that it is impossible for a man and a woman to be simply friends – and that your best opposite-sex friend will inevitably take on the role of a boyfriend or girlfriend, stopping you from meeting the person you are supposed to be with. The way she put it was:

> 'What if you spend a lot of time together, and one evening you have some vino and you're play-fighting, and then you get play wrestling, and then you're kissing, and before you know it you're getting it on . . .'

I strongly disagree with this. If you put your boundaries in place (and importantly, don't drink too much 'vino'!), it just isn't going to happen. I think the benefits of having healthy, normalized other-sex friendships far outweigh the potential problems. So long as you know what you are looking for and what God wants for you – see your seven standards; you can only benefit from having friends of the opposite gender. Also keep your boundaries. Warm, supportive friendship does not mean play fighting or wrestling matches!

The start of a beautiful relationship?

The other thing to remember is that, like Andy and Helen, friendship can be the start of a beautiful relationship for some couples. You can't count on it by any means, but I do know of several cases where things have worked out that way. And even if you don't start off as friends – you just launch straight into dating – it will still go that way eventually because if you don't have a good friendship, mutual respect, enjoyment of each other's company, and things in common, it won't last, or you will be miserable.

One wise friend of mine from university said this to me when I was bemoaning my lack of relationship success:

> 'It's really not that complicated, Becky – they should just be the one person who you like to spend time with more than anyone else; who you like more than anyone else.'

However, some friendships can get blurry if both parties are single and you are not careful.

For example . . . the Interim Boyfriend phenomenon.

I believe that the Interim 'Boyfriend' or 'Girlfriend' is a very common situation. This is someone who you like, but for various reasons do not get together with. They do not carry out all the same functions, but they do fulfil the role in many respects. You spend time together, flirt, go for walks, cook together . . . and then one of

I believe that the Interim 'Boyfriend' or 'Girlfriend' is a very common situation

you gets a real partner and 'blam!' you suddenly realize that you don't want things to change. Not that you would or could really have been with your interim – otherwise you would have got together. But that's not the point – you were partners in crime, you were both enjoying your singleness together, having fun and now suddenly they have been taken away from you. No wonder you feel a sense of loss – even when it is mixed with happiness that your friend has found love.

So how do you deal with this? It is a tricky one, and depends on how close you were to your interim. Things will definitely change between you now that he or she is paired up; they have to really – you can't carry on as you were. But that doesn't mean you will stop being friends. The answer is to concentrate on the positive things that you can still have with your friend. Friendship is amazing and beautiful and enriching; and you can still cherish that – whether your friendship is over or just entering a different phase.

I have seen so many of my friends go through this and I've been through it myself a couple of times. I think the reason it is so common is that all good relationships have friendship at the heart of them as well as attraction. They must have this basis, because in the end everything goes saggy, wrinkly and misshapen. If you are basing your relationship solely on looks you are heading for a crash! This being so, of course, your opposite-gender relationships can get confusing from time to time. You are going to have to accept and deal with that as it goes in your particular story. It is worth it for the good times you will have and the things you will learn for when you find the partner God has in store for you.

Action! A brave step

Look at your friendship group, and ask whether there is someone within it who might be right for you. If so, consider taking the very brave step of asking them out.

Tip: Only do this after careful consideration, and certainly only do it with one friend in the group, not all of the men or all of the women. Otherwise you will get a reputation!

PART IV

GO!

In which a few of the less helpful aspects of the church's attitude towards single people are examined, and in which I try to reassure you that you are not alone and it is time to get dating!

20

BEING SINGLE IN THE CHURCH

'Singleness is a gift. You should cherish it'

I now want to write a little bit to those of you who have read this far and are still not sure whether it is Biblical to date as prolifically as I have done during this research. Hopefully this will persuade you that there is nothing wrong with active searching. The fact is that things are not working at the moment for single people in the church, to the extent that some people think we are actually losing people from church because of this issue. One of the reasons for this could be our own attitudes, whether we are single or paired up.

Church is about God first, which is as it should be. The second biggest thing in church is often community – it's about sharing the good things of life together, as a big happy family. That's how it is when it's working, and it's great. I've been there – I've celebrated with the families, the old people, the children and young couples. I'm sure in church you also have your close friends, your acquaintances, elders who mentor you, kids who run around your legs and make you spill your coffee . . . and so the list goes on. You can't flourish as a Christian alone – you need the support and encouragement of others.

However, sometimes, if you are single, being with your fellow Christians can feel like the loneliest place on earth. Especially if no-one talks about your singleness, or if they don't seem to understand how things look through your single spectacles. And in spite of the silence you find in some congregations, often people have a great deal to say on the subject of singleness in the church and there are some strong opinions around. Here are a few choice bits of advice that might sound familiar:

- ♥ 'Dating isn't God's way – it's the world's way.'
- ♥ 'You should just wait and see.'
- ♥ 'Don't do *those* holidays – that's not the right way to meet someone.' (The same goes for *those* websites, *those* clubs, *those* parties, etc.)
- ♥ 'You should just look within your church – "the one" is probably right under your nose!'
- ♥ 'Singleness is a gift – you should cherish it while you have it.' (This one is invariably said by married people.)
- ♥ 'Maybe God wants you to be alone – you can do more for him if you aren't tied down.'
- ♥ 'Maybe you just want it too much. I feel it has become an idol in your life – above God. He won't bless you with a relationship until you make it less of a priority.'
- ♥ 'You should stop dating and wait for God's timing.'
- ♥ 'When you meet the right person, you will just know. God will make it clear.'

These are all real bits of advice that I have heard at some time or another from friends. If I'm honest, most of these made me feel pretty rotten and somewhat confused. This advice may have been given with the best of intentions. It may have been meant for a season, not forever. It may even have some truth within it. But to the ears of a person who has been single and waiting for years it does not sound like an encouragement. It sounds like a slap-down.

How will I 'just know' when the right guy comes along?

And some of it just sounds downright crazy and impractical. I'm not a particularly impulsive decision maker. How will I 'just know' when the right guy comes along? Is he going to be shining with some kind of heavenly preternatural glow? Will he be just so darned *nice* that I know he's the one? Will he ask me to marry him on date number two?

Of course I want to find someone to love and start a new chapter in life with. A lot. Should I feel bad about this? Should I squash it down inside myself and deny it?

At one point I asked myself these questions in earnest. Perhaps this was what I should be doing. Maybe I was supposed to stop wanting love and a family? Maybe this was the way forward? One day, after an especially choice bit of advice, I asked myself and God – so, is Becky Maddox 'Called To Be Single'? (The dreaded phrase!)

And the answer came from God perfectly clearly and quickly: 'No! Maybe it's right for some people, but not for you, my girl! I've got someone great lined up for you, but there are just a few things that you need to do for me first and a few red herrings too . . .'

God knows the desires of your heart, and he gives you those desires for a reason. It is a well-worn phrase, but it is still true. I really think that *not* to pursue those goals and dreams would be going against God. The way I see it, for anything to happen in this life some sort of action

Even couples who insist that God brought them together must have made some kind of decision

must be taken. Even couples who insist that God brought them together and showed them in a moment that 'this was it' must have made some kind of decision or taken action at some point, even if it was just plucking up the courage to say hello and find out the other person's name.

So if one of your heartfelt desires is to fall in love or one of your goals is to start a family then go after your dreams today – don't waste any time! As a busy friend once said to me, 'Quite frankly, if I don't put it on my to-do list pretty soon it's never going to get done!' This particular friend always does everything on her 'to-do' list, so I know if she puts it on there it will happen. We're not all able to get through those dreaded lists, but at least if it's on the list it at least stands a chance!

I would love to see more Christians putting 'find life partner' on their to-do list, getting out on the dating scene and meeting potential partners in a proactive but relaxed way – a way that's going to lead them to a soul mate they can stick with happily ever after. A way that isn't rushed and over-eager, but calm, thoughtful, genuine and Godly. A way that is based on shared interests and a shared outlook on life – not the fact that your friends and family like them, or the idea that you won't do any better so you'd better lock this one down quick, or the fact that they are really attractive and you really want sex!

Matchmaker, matchmaker . . .

The other side of the coin is the matchmaking that often goes on in church. I have known some pretty prolific matchmakers in my time. More often than not, matchmaking doesn't work, and frequently the results are spectacularly and disastrously off track. If you think about it, it is hard enough to buy clothes or jewellery to match someone's taste, so no wonder it is hard to pick someone a life partner. In spite of the disastrous outcomes, most matchmaking efforts are done with the best of intentions and love for the people involved.

I think churches can be a bit like this. My church is a hotbed of well-intentioned gossip and speculation when it comes to relations between the sexes. Very often if a young unmarried man and woman start to talk to each other after the service on a Sunday, looking out for each other, paying special attention to one another – it will be noticed and talked about. Suggestions might be made, or hints dropped, to the pair in question, even in front of other people. No matter how well-meant, this can backfire and make the two people involved feel deeply uncomfortable. If there is any burgeoning feeling between them, it might be squashed by all the attention from outside.

It can get mighty claustrophobic and unreal when you are in a church like this. You are not sure whether to strike up a friendship with a new girl or guy in case they misinterpret it, or you do, or the whole of the rest of the church does. In fact, I have found it really hard to form deep friendships with the opposite sex within my church. That's why I find my friendships with men outside my own church so precious and sustaining.

21

'DOT' THEORY

'To the world you may be one person, but to one person you may be the world'

Now I have a question for you: do you believe there is a person ready and waiting for you – just the one, the right one for you? Or do you think there are several 'ones' who you could find and create a relationship with?

There is a theory going round in some Christian circles called 'dot' theory. This theory suggests that there is one perfect person out there who God has got lined up for you, and when you meet that person everything will just slot into place and become clear. All well and good – and maybe true.

Except what if someone's spouse dies young? Or someone else's wife leaves? Or, less seriously perhaps, what if two people date one another for a short while and one of them decides that it isn't right?

Should those people be on their own forever because they have already met one person and it didn't work out?

Working it out

Here's another question for you: do you believe that God has got one particular job, or a series of jobs lined up for you? Or has God made you capable of doing many jobs that you could do equally well to his glory?

For some reason, this second question doesn't feel quite as controversial as the first. Why is that?

We could get into a big debate here about the theology of choice, chance and predestination, but I'm not going to do that. I'm simply going to observe that things are not always clear-cut in life, and it is a lie to suggest that they are. A lot of it is about the choices and decisions we make and the way we choose to react to things. So if you are feeling tentative about who you want to spend the rest of your life with then don't worry; it's perfectly normal, and don't let anyone tell you otherwise! Marriage is a massive step to take after all.

So if you are feeling tentative about who you want to spend the rest of your life with then don't worry; it's perfectly normal

In the end, I do believe God has got everything lined up – he's God – how can he not? But he doesn't want to tell you the ending before you get there! Also, his plans sometimes differ from ours – every Christian knows this from experience.

Maybe you do know exactly who you are and where you are going in every area of your life. Some people are blessed with this – they know exactly what job they are meant to do, they know exactly which relationship they should be in, when to get married, when to have children, when to retire, when to check into the nursing home and when to take their last breath. But for most of us life simply isn't like that. It's not something we should blame ourselves for; it just is what it is.

Life is frequently about living in a moment of doubt, and making the most of that moment. I think as Christians we can look back along our lives and see where God has been in action. However, as we are actually living our lives it can feel a lot messier, more complicated and less clear than when we look back.

And here's another thing: not knowing where you are going at the beginning of a relationship does not mean you are not listening to God enough. It just means that you are figuring it out – and there is nothing at all wrong with that.

In fact, dot theory taken to the extreme can be very damaging. I am sure that thinking 'is this the one?' after the first date has jeopardized or destroyed many perfectly good potential relationships. Even thinking it on the third date can freeze one or both parties with fear so that the relationship dies on the tree. How do I know? I've been there.

I worry about people who subscribe to dot theory: the idea that they will 'just know' when they meet 'the one'. I fear they are likely to be extreme – either marrying their first boyfriend or girlfriend ill-advisedly at a very young age and spending the rest of their lives trying to figure out what they are doing with this person; or not meeting anyone at all, sitting at home unchanging, pining, with nothing happening. The latter are the ones who are unwilling to take any kind of action or try anything because they think it should Just Happen.

If you are one of those people, I've got news for you: it isn't going to Just Happen. You have to do something. You have to try. Here's a dating tale about just giving it a try.

Trying is better than not

So there I was with several hours to kill before my evening date. I was in a little village in Hertfordshire called Markyate and I was going to the pantomime . . . on Valentine's Day.

My date for the evening was Dave. He is a friend of my friend Jess, so this was a prearranged classic blind-date; a set-up. And I was nervous. I kept wondering, 'What if we don't get on? What will I say to Jess? How will I tell her I think he is boring or bigheaded?' Then, 'What if we *do* get on, but it doesn't work out?'

These were the thoughts that were churning in my head as I wandered around Markyate. The sun was out and the last remnants of snow were clinging to the pavements, looking like a scab ready to be picked off. Markyate was a proper old village. There was a bakery, an 'Olde Village Post Office', a butcher, three pubs and a cute little café. I started my long wait in the café. Inside, two sets of parents were trying to get their kids to kiss each other because it was Valentine's Day. They were resistant to this and the little boy ran away crying. Some early matchmaking trauma – a presentiment of tonight, maybe?

Inside, two sets of parents were trying to get their kids to kiss each other and the little boy ran away crying

I have to say, for the first time I could remember, I was barely aware that it was Valentine's Day. I wasn't looking out for cards on the doormat in the morning. I held out no hopes of special romantic treatment. And this actually made me feel strangely free. I sipped my coffee and read my book.

After a time the café closed. I decided a drink would be a good idea to steady the nerves so picked one of the three pubs and strode confidently in. Inside it was SCARY – really tiny and really local. It felt like stepping into someone's house. When I walked through the door all heads turned. 'Boom-boom-boom-boom, I want you in my room' was playing on the jukebox. Everyone in there seemed to know each other.

I approached the bar. After a short wait the barman appeared from outside; a plump man with flushed cheeks.

'Sorry about that,' he said breathlessly. 'The chickens were just being released.'

'Where to?' I asked.

'To their natural habitat.'

The barman started telling me about a particular chicken called Les. I nodded and smiled as best I could, ordered pear cider, retreated to a corner and pretended to read my book.

At 4 p.m. I got a text from my friend Annie who was in the matinee with her daughter.

'It is two hours into the show and Jack hasn't even gone up the beanstalk yet . . .'

It was going to be a long night.

Then Atheist Andy texted saying that he was in a cosy house watching a big TV – was I jealous? I texted back: 'Not jealous. Am in a pub drinking pear cider and gathering experiences. You can be happy with your big TV, I am happy with my pantomime.'

The pantomime

At that moment I had a thought – maybe caused by the progress I was making into my second pint of pear cider, but anyhow . . . It suddenly struck me that this whole dating game is a bit of a pantomime really. Here we all are, dancing around each other – back and forth – flirting and hoping, praying, ducking and darting.

It is a big old performance.

Until you meet the right one I suppose.

And that's when the pantomime becomes even more prominent and important. In a long relationship there must be days, weeks, even months, when you don't feel like loving that person, when you just can't be bothered to make the effort – but you do. Those are the panto days that really count in making a relationship last. Choosing to act the love you don't feel until it comes back again. Acting it and hoping it will return with more depth and maturity than before. Giving the other person what they need, not what you feel like giving them or think they deserve. Maybe a bit of panto can be a good thing.

I was brought out of my philosophical reverie by the realization that the locals were going behind the bar and helping themselves to the drinks. A group of small children had also entered the pub and were running amuck everywhere, being chased by a well-built person called 'Uncle Steve' – a large jolly man who couldn't run fast enough to catch any of them. 'He's had two pasties and a steak slice today!' squawked his wife and they all fell about laughing.

Their banter filled the room, snippets of conversations:

'Rugby's in 25 minutes.'

'What time we booked in for? I'm starving.'

'He's had two pasties and a steak slice today!' squawked his wife and they all fell about laughing

'Music change, please, Les.'

Tinny happy-60s pop filled the room.

'Yeah – Carpenters! Carpenters is wicked – great tune, man!'

The last speaker was Uncle Steve and he started dancing around the room with children hanging off him. Beside the bar a couple stood watching this scene, not saying a word, apparently bored by each other, the pub and the whole situation. But then he reached over and stroked the back of her hand, smiling, and their quiet contentment showed. I nursed my pear cider and smiled too, feeling one of those strange moments of perfection that suddenly come out of nowhere – happy in the moment.

Invisible reasons

Well, in the end, my long wait for the date with Dave was worth it. The pantomime was great fun. I couldn't help being won over by the jollity and the sheer good-nature of it all – even during the really bad jokes (of which there weren't too many). In fact there were some really good ones.

It was the same with my date, Dave. I couldn't help being won over by him and his sweet good nature either. We got on very well indeed. There was plenty to talk about and the couple of hours we spent sharing a curry flew by. We did have to dash at the end as Dave was doing the lighting for the pantomime. I think the waiter was a little taken aback by us whisking out of the door at 7 p.m., but he still managed to thrust a single red rose into my hand, which was nice . . . if a little odd, as I then had to carry it for the rest of the evening. Perhaps I should have flung it at the end of the show when Jack, his mother, the cow and the beanstalk took their bow, but I didn't think of it at the time.

Dave was lovely, yes. Not tingly, but lovely. I would probably have gone out with him again if he had asked me but he never did. He didn't seem like the type of guy to ask you out on a second date even if he liked you.

So 'Why did the date happen at all then?' I hear you dating sceptics cry . . . If it was never going to go anywhere, why bother spending an evening together somewhere? There are two possible answers to this.

The first is very straightforward – you never know until you try! It is as simple as that. Dave and I might have been made for each other. It turns out that we were not, but we would never have had this information if we hadn't gone out for a (perfectly enjoyable) curry together.

The second is more complex. As a Christian I do believe that everything happens for a reason. But I do not translate this into meaning any or all of the following:

1. I only need to go on one date in my life in order to find 'the one'.
2. That date will be with Mr Right.
3. We will know it from the first ten minutes of meeting and he will propose within the week.

This is 'dot theory' and I think it is pure fantasy, on a par with a young man climbing up a giant beanstalk and finding a goose that lays golden eggs.

However, I do think there are reasons why my date with Dave happened. One possibility is that God wanted Dave to start dating so that he could meet the right one. Maybe it was a wake-up call for Dave? Or maybe it was a reminder to me that the quieter or less forthcoming guys can have great potential . . . Who knows? I'll leave those details to God. All I know is that I don't regret giving it a go. In the end Dave and I went on a date to find out a bit more about each other. We found out that we got on well, but are not meant to be together. Which is fine.

It can hurt, but failed relationships can be learnt from and turned into knowledge

I think the whole point of dating is to meet a variety of people, find out who you are as well as who your perfect partner might be, and eventually settle down with someone who is right for you. It needn't be complex. It can hurt, but failed relationships can be learnt from and turned into knowledge.

Action!

Why not have a go at being set up for a blind date?

I know it sounds potentially awkward and cringy – but think about it. Your friends know you really well – all your foibles and sparkly plus points. They have your best interests at heart and they really care about you. If they choose someone for you, the chances are that they will choose really well. So – make a list of two or three close friends who know you really well and might know some eligible bachelors or bachelorettes, give them your list of seven standards (see chapter 18) and ask them to set you up. What have you got to lose?

22

WHAT IS THE CHURCH UP TO?

'A lady's imagination is very rapid; it jumps from admiration to love, from love to matrimony in a moment'
– Jane Austen

This book is based on the idea that we are made to be in community and God's plan for us is that we should be in relationship with each other. The human being is a social animal – moreover we are made to mate for life. The desire for pair-bonding is rooted deep in our genes, in our hearts. It goes back to the beginning of time, to the pre-history of the Garden where the snake mucked it all up for Adam and Eve.

The strange thing is that very few people in church are talking about the number of single people in our congregations. How many sermons do you hear that have stories or examples taken from single life? Is no-one aware of the single people in our midst? Is it that people forget how it feels to be single once they are married? Is everyone assuming that single people are content in their singleness, so there is nothing to worry about and therefore nothing to be done?

Twenties and thirties

A while ago I moved house and was looking for a new church to go to in the area. I was pretty thorough in my search and visited about six different places altogether. At every church I visited I went to the newcomers meeting when we would be taken through the ethos of the church and all the different areas that you could get involved in:

- Welcome team
- Stewarding
- Children's work
- Mothers' group
- Marriage preparation
- Family services
- Home groups
- Women's group
- Men's group

But where were the single people activities? When I asked the question I was frequently met with confusion or silence, or sometimes with the phrase 'twenties and thirties'. We all know that 'twenties and thirties' is a euphemism for single people. If there is a twenties and thirties group in the church it is invariably full of singletons: some of them perfectly happy, some of them a bit unhappy, but not very many of them openly dating.

The quiet approach

A friend of mine went on at least one Oak Hall holiday every year, and she had been doing it since she was fifteen. For those of you who are complete initiates to Oak

Hall, this is a Christian holiday company which runs trips to all sorts of places from Israel to Bahrain to Bognor. It is not explicitly for single people, but it certainly attracts a lot. The hidden subtext is very important here. Even though Oak Hall does not market itself as being for single people, it is well known that it is, even to the point of earning the nickname 'Bloke Pull'!

After fifteen years of going away every summer and every winter, she finally met a man

Every time my friend went away she would insist that she wasn't going on these holidays to try and meet someone. After fifteen years of going away every summer and every winter, she finally met a man. She came home on the plane wreathed in smiles and full of her news. And the idea that the Oak Hall holidays were purely for having fun and making friends was thrown out of the window!

I'm glad that my friend has found someone and that they are both happy. But why did she hide her hopes of finding a man? Was she ashamed of looking? Was she genuinely not looking? Did she not dare to hope that something might come of it, so she never mentioned it?

This friend is a very chatty person – one of the most talkative I know. But whenever the subject of being single came up she would go strangely quiet. Even now she doesn't talk too much about her man, which shows wisdom that I respect. They are still finding out about each other. And yet, even Ruth was doing something about it in her quiet way when she laid herself at Boaz's feet – and it paid off!

Saying what you hope for

As an aside, why is it that we single people in the church sometimes find it difficult to have an identity, or to confess that we would like to find someone? Perhaps we don't want to express our desire in case it seems ungrateful to God. After all, he has provided so much already – should we really be asking for a relationship as well? Maybe we are actually deeply scared that we won't meet anyone and that by opening our mouths to express that desire we might inadvertently stop it from ever happening. Or maybe we don't feel that we deserve love – that we have done something that makes us essentially unlovable.

There was a time when I thought like this. I fell mostly into the category of not wanting to seem ungrateful, with a bit of feeling that I didn't deserve to be loved. Then I realized that God loves and forgives completely and unconditionally. Actually I do deserve love, and moreover I believe it is part of God's plan for me to be with someone one day, and he wants me to have a good time finding him, stop worrying and encourage other people on the same journey!

Sometimes we forget that God is a good and gracious father

Sometimes we forget that God is a good and gracious father. He is not cruel and he does not withhold good things from his children. Part of expressing my faith is to pursue God's promises to me. One of those promises is that I might one day love, be loved, marry and have a family. So by dating, I'm doing my best to be open to that happening in a positive, Godly and active way.

Of course, it isn't always easy to stay positive when nothing is working out; but I find it is an act of faith to keep looking, even when things have gone wrong and hurts have come along. During this search some things have happened that have made me want to give up looking – to pack it all in and say enough is enough. But I've come to realize that it is a better act of faith to keep going than to withdraw from the search, because it shows that I trust God will make it right in the end.

Stand up and be counted!

So, I am inspired by my friend's quiet patience and perseverance. But I also think there is sometimes a place for being loud about being single in church as well.

I would like to see churches where singleness is discussed openly from the front, where examples are used in sermons from the lives of single people, not just from family life. I am not sure whether this will ever happen, because couples and families are often placed above single people in many church societies.

A step forward would be to have some groups or activities for single people – such as social evenings, coffee house meet-ups or special services if it's a big church. Something more relaxed than the 'home group' model, which is usually an enclave of earnest Bible study. A social secretary in each church could organize everything.

And what about inter-church seeking? Most churches are small, with only a hundred or so members. In a church like that, you will quickly know whether or not there is a potential spouse lurking on the back pew or not. And if not, what do you do then? It would be great if the social secretary of the twenties and thirties group were to keep an eye out for events happening in the area and organize people to go along, or even get in touch with social secretaries from other churches and arrange something together.

Some friends of mine started up a Facebook group for twenties and thirties Christians in Milton Keynes called Gridlife. Anyone from any church in the area could join the Facebook group – chat, post events, discuss aspects of Christian life. You didn't have to be single, just in your twenties and thirties. Every month or so there was a meet-up. It was a great initiative.

These things are often happening at churches in an informal way – so why is it not mentioned in the welcome pack, or the newsletter? I find this extremely interesting . . . When I asked the question at my old church I was told that people don't like to go along to activities or events that are advertised as being for single people.

I found this extraordinary. Why? Why be embarrassed about going along to an event for single people? Singleness is nothing to be ashamed of. It is just a state, a season of life. I am neither ashamed nor proud of my single state. It is what it is. However, I am keen to meet someone and not worried who knows that. Does that make me odd or sensible? You decide!

Finally, what about the potential of experienced mentors in the church helping people to find partners? I'm not saying that the vicar should be openly matchmaking – that probably wouldn't be appropriate. But a little subtle behind-the-scenes work by the pastoral team or elders might do no harm. Having said this, it needs to be done in the right way so as not to cause embarrassment. Churches can be very gossipy places, as discussed earlier!

If we are serious about finding someone suitable, thoughtful, sensitive matchmaking with the full permission of the people involved is, I believe, a valid method. When I began researching this book, I asked my home group leaders to look out for potential men to date. I have been on several dates following on from a recommendation, some of which you have read about. I have also offered the same matchmaking service to some of my shyer and less forthcoming friends. Some of them say yes, some no. So far I have only had one matchmaking success but maybe there are more ahead . . . Anyway, I would encourage you to use all your contacts and start finding out who is out there.

So far I have only had one matchmaking success but maybe there are more ahead . . .

Action! Twenties, thirties and flirties!

What does your church do for the single people in your congregation? Have you ever asked the question? Of course it might be risky to ask. It frequently happens that asking such a question will lead to you being invited to take on the responsibility of starting and running such a group for yourself. But maybe you should pray about it and take up the challenge.

And what about the potential for inter-church mingling? Could you try setting up a Facebook group to meet a wider range of Christians in your area?

Why not try a Christian holiday? As part of my research, I went on an Oak Hall Bible Weekend and had a thoroughly good time. I also met a lovely couple who had recently got married after meeting on one of the holidays. So it can work.

23

GET MOVING!

'Do you want to know who you are? Don't ask. Act! Action will delineate and define you.'
– Thomas Jefferson

This is just a short chapter to all the lazy lovers out there. You know who you are, so I'm not going to 'go on' at you too much. But I do just have a few words for all of you who are dipping your toe into the dating pool, but not quite taking the plunge (for whatever reason).

The fact is that if you sit on your hands forever, or only dabble on the edges of actually dating people, you will never meet anyone. No matter how good looking, charming, witty and delightful you are – nobody is ever going to fall for you.

You will simply be sitting at home forever, looking good and telling yourself hilarious jokes. Which is fine, if that's what you want. But if you'd rather be telling your hilarious jokes to an audience for life, you are going to have to take some risks.

In the end, it is an act of selflessness to step outside your front door and go on a date. Why? Because you are willing to share that sparkling, funny and intriguing you. You are willing to pack your self-consciousness away for an evening and go and entertain someone. You are willing to go on an adventure, to look outside yourself, and take a chance. God will honour that, and also you are honouring yourself by putting yourself out there.

Do not

My own experience of the extreme caution that dating seems to produce in some Christian men was interesting. As I began my experimental search I become increasingly surprised by how utterly unmotivated many of the men I encountered were, especially considering the fact that I was meeting them on dating sites and at singles parties. They were clearly looking for someone and intent on finding them, otherwise they wouldn't be there.

Many took my number, or made interested noises, but then balked at the first meet-up. Now perhaps this is because I simply didn't inspire them to be motivated – maybe they just didn't fancy me, which is fine. But I'm pretty sure that at least one of them might have liked me. So why the complete lack of chutzpah?!

Many took my number, or made interested noises, but then balked at the first meet-up

For example, one guy, Mark, and I chatted for ages on the Web, got to know a lot about each other, seemed to be into similar things and on the same wavelength. After a few messages I suggested a meet-up to see whether we hit it off in the flesh too. But as soon as I suggested this he prevaricated and procrastinated and avoided. He just wasn't willing to step out of his comfort zone enough to actually meet me. So I gave up, asking myself what on earth he was doing on that website if he wasn't capable of meeting another human being in real life.

That might have been a great loss for both of us. But we will never know.

If you are an Internet dater (or any other kind of dater) who has a phobia of actually meeting with someone of the opposite sex, try looking at it this way: if you can't commit to an initial meeting with someone, how on earth are you going to be able to commit to a marriage? (I'm assuming that's what most readers of this book are looking for ultimately.) Also, ask yourself: how exactly are you planning on meeting 'the one' if you are afraid to even leave the house?

So, I suggest a change of mindset for us – men and women alike. Get out there and start meeting people in real life settings – don't take it so seriously or expect to meet 'the one' on your first date, but keep that in mind as the ultimate goal. Above all, don't give up (they are just people after all).

Do?

Then there are the men I did manage to meet up with and who were lovely and chatty but just acted like I was their friend and never made a move of any sort. There were a couple of guys like that. One in particular I was chatting to and meeting up with for about six months and I eventually assumed that he only saw me as a friend, because I didn't have the smallest hint that it might be otherwise. Now I think of him as a friend and nothing else because he has entered the friend zone.

At least you know, so you can get on with your life

It might have been otherwise, but I am not a mind-reader.

As the old saying goes, 'faint heart never won fair lady', and it is as true today as it ever was. If you are keen on someone, try to let them know sooner rather than later. Maybe not directly after the first date – but do find an appropriate time reasonably early if possible. An early declaration of intent will save a lot of heartache in the future, stop a lot of time wasting, and clear up misunderstandings. You never know, they might feel the same way and bingo – you are sorted. And if not? Well at least you know, so you can get on with your life.

Now, I'm not saying it should always be the man who makes the move, but experience has shown me that this can work better. Large and obvious hints can be dropped, but there is something about the man being in pursuit that is still appropriate.

Having said this, there are times when it is better to keep your feelings to yourself, and even to run from them. If the object of your affection is trying to get over a failed relationship or an unrequited love it is probably not the best time to leap into declaring your love, as you will more than likely be rejected, plus it will make it difficult, if not impossible, for you to support your friend through their tough time. It is quite a selfish way to behave, really, to announce yourself at a time like that.

If the person you like is involved with someone else then you should certainly not say anything. You should readjust your head immediately. And if you can't readjust your head, you need to get out of their company until you are over them. It just isn't wise to feed a crush like that.

But if you are both free and single (not necessarily young) – then what on earth are you waiting for?

In the end, it doesn't matter if the first date fails, or even if the third, fifth or seventh date fails, because at least you DID!

So declare your intentions, get dating and get moving.

And have fun too!

24

COURTSHIP AND COMMITMENT

'Courtship consists in a number of quiet attentions, not so pointed as to alarm, nor so vague as not to be understood'
– Laurence Sterne

Although this book is mainly about dating – the experiences, opportunities and fun you can have meeting the right person for you – the background theme has always been setting out on the big journey of courtship ending in marriage, or 'forever'. The reason you are dating at all is to meet someone and fall in lasting love with them. Here are a few tips for the first stages of the relationship when you do meet someone you hope might be 'the one'.

So there you are. You have been on three tremendously successful dates and you are 100 per cent sure that you want to continue with the relationship – or at least you are between 51 per cent and 99 per cent sure (I would be very surprised if you were 100 per cent). You have decided that you are sure enough to start a serious relationship with this person – aiming towards marriage. Once you have been on three dates and are considering moving from dating to courtship, forever is not inevitable but it is a possibility. You have looked this possibility squarely in the eye, decided you would be very happy with that outcome and are ploughing onwards. Good for you!

Be prepared for things to go wrong or seem difficult

Now you have to be bold enough to stand by that decision, it is time to make it 'official' and to start to build them into your life. Introduce them to your friends and family. Get them involved in all the different aspects of your life. Keep communication open, clear and regular. Be particularly vigilant about the last point if you live far away from your beloved and are a busy person. In short, create a plan of action and stick to it as a priority in your life.

Be prepared for things to go wrong or seem difficult. At times the integration of two lives can seem like hard work. Even if your intended is perfection itself, it can be nerve-wracking introducing him or her to people, especially to members of your family – because families are rarely perfect. As time goes on, you will also discover that your partner is not perfect either. There will be things about them that you are not so keen on. They will surprise you at times, infuriate you, make you sad or cross. None of these are reasons to dump the other person – they are challenges for you to work through together, and they are part of the sometimes uncomfortable process of learning to love another. It is all about readjustment.

Don't try to change them, but be ready to change together

If you are with someone, and you love them but think they are going to change in certain ways through your influence, then you had better drop that notion quickly. Love is not about trying to shape or mould the other person into what you want them to be, or thinking that they will change in the way you want them to. You need to take it as read that they won't change. The person that you see before you today is the one that you will be with forever. You must wholeheartedly love and accept them already, as they are, without expectation – or you will be disappointed.

Having said this, it is almost inevitable that over the months and years of being together you will influence each other. So rather than planning how you will change the other, you need to be ready to change yourself, adapt and compromise. This kind of change is very different to yielding under pressure from the other person. It is about wanting to change because you love the other person; you have a heartfelt desire to do and be the best you can for them. It is a willing choice – moulding and shaping doesn't come into it.

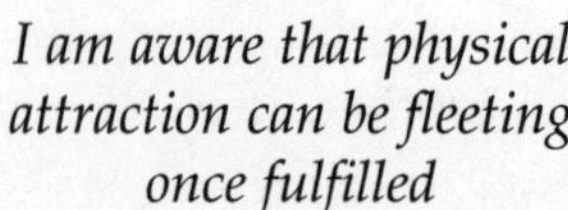

I am aware that physical attraction can be fleeting once fulfilled

In the end, a partnership should be about helping and supporting each other to be the best that you both can be – to be everything God made you for, and doing this selflessly with the very best interests of the other at heart. Ultimately, love is an action not a feeling, and it is in the action of how you treat the other person daily that your love will make itself felt and known, becoming strong.

Keep your pants on

OK, I will be brief here. (D'you get it – brief? Briefs? No? Oh well, never mind!) Basically, if you are aiming for the gold standard of no-sex-before-marriage, this is going to be one of the biggest challenges you will face with your new serious boyfriend or girlfriend. I hesitate to write this in some ways because I know that I have fallen short in this area before. Also, I am aware that physical attraction can be fleeting once fulfilled, and that couples who get married because of this initial deep attraction might find themselves in difficulties. However, I still strongly believe that sex is sacred and a gift to be treasured, not undertaken lightly or messed about with. Your eagerness to hop into bed can show how much you value yourself as a person.

The ultimate standard of this is to keep all sexual activity out of relationships until marriage. So, with this in mind, here are my . . .

Top ways to postpone sex

Try these and add some more of your own if you like . . .

1. Draw the boundaries before the opportunity to cross over them arises. That way you will have planned exactly how you are going to react and nothing will take you by surprise. So for example, on a first date

you will allow a brief hug and peck on the cheek; on a fourth date one short kiss, etc.

2. Don't go to their house or your own for dates – go to public places.
3. Don't tidy your bedroom, so that you are embarrassed to take him or her in there (maybe this one is a bit extreme).
4. Always wear big, unattractive or holey (even holy) underpants whenever he or she is around.
5. Strip your bed before he or she comes round so that it is unmade and uninviting.
6. Have friends around when you go on dates.
7. Hold yourself accountable to someone sympathetic.
8. Agree your boundaries with your partner and stick to them. If you are getting close to the edge, simply do something else. Get up off the sofa or bed and go out to somewhere where you can't follow the course of action you have begun.

By having these rules and standards you will give yourself the best chance of honouring your decision, God, yourself and your partner.

Look outwards

As you court, try not to focus too much on each other. It can be tricky, when all you can think of is him or her – how wonderful they are, how clever, how good-looking, how happy they make you feel, that they share your passion for kick-boxing in heels, etc., etc. But eventually the other things in your life will come crowding back in and it is right and healthy that they do, otherwise the pair of you are just a floating island – of no use to anybody else in the world.

So I would really encourage you to make community part of your courtship. Being part of a group together (church or some other social group) is so important, as are the activities you do together and time spent as a couple with family or other friends.

The 'M' word

So, how do you know that something is going in the right direction; and what if you are worried about marriage, worried about the 'not knowing', worried about wasting your precious time and emotion?

It is a nerve-wracking thing, embarking on a relationship. The truth is that neither of you knows for sure that it will work out, and yet you must operate in an atmosphere of trusting and believing that it will.

It is a nerve-wracking thing, embarking on a relationship

First of all, don't panic.

Secondly, relax and take stock. See what stage your relationship is at. If you're only a couple of months in, just shelve that question for a later date and go with the flow. If you are a couple of years in it is a very different matter . . . You definitely need to address the issue. And when you are engaged? Not that much will change. It is still a nerve-wracking thing, embarking on a marriage. It's just a whole new and different set of issues to those you faced as a single person (or so I am reliably informed!).

PART V

WRAPPING IT UP

In which I attempt to come to a
Conclusion of Consequence

25

LOVING GOD FIRST

'Whatever your heart clings to and confides in, that is really your God'
– Martin Luther, 1483–1546, German theologian

So there we are. As a result of my research I went to gigs, stand-up comedy shows, restaurants and London Zoo. I was almost compromised on the dance floor, stranded in a muddy village and the catcher of a bouquet. I sheltered under a cupcake box, waited nervously in line for results and spent hours trawling profiles on the Internet. I was driven in a rusty car with no floor and chased by an angry granny. I narrowly escaped a squirting tiger and a falling pigeon, attempted to eat a variety of difficult foodstuffs while trying to look attractive, and struggled in and out of my glad rags in the toilets of approximately ten trains to London. I was confused, amused, frustrated and dazzled by wedding rings on the fingers of attractive men. But overall I laughed a lot more than I cried.

In some ways I failed because I only managed to go on fourteen successful dates as a result of my research:

Simon – the man with a life
Joe – the man in the hat

John – the unforthcoming one (who never made a romantic move)
Lawrence – the one with no confidence
James – the gorilla king
Eduardo – the over-ardent
Richard – the pigeon disaster man
Milos – the oversexed
Nush – the snowman
Dave – the panto man
Tony – the unwitting friend
Imma – the text maniac
Mike – the toxic bachelor
Tomas – the Hungarian biochemist

. . . and had six near-misses . . .

Max – the taken Facebook man
Mark – the Internet dater who couldn't bear to meet up
Chris – the Christmas curry man
Tony – the married pastor
Sam – the one at the wedding who took fright at my bouquet-catching skills

Oh yes, and the cautious bookworm whose name I never discovered.

I am excluding the carpenter of Milton Keynes and the part-time Eskimo from this list as one was 70 and the other was incoherent . . . though perhaps if things get really desperate . . .

I also failed to find a steady boyfriend, but at least I tried!

I also failed to find a steady boyfriend, but at least I tried!

Most importantly of all, I made some new friends (and no enemies).

Missing from the list?

The best dates that I went on during my research were the ones where I kept God close. I didn't always do this, sometimes forgetting because I got caught up in attraction or the excitement of the chase. But it always worked better when I asked God to be involved.

Throughout this time of going on lots of dates and meeting lots of men, I have also tried to make it a habit to romance God on a regular basis: to get away with him and be alone – just the two of us; to anchor myself in him firmly so that the storms and sunny days of the search do not shake me too much. When I meet with God I can meet with triumph or disaster and treat those two imposters just the same. You could do this too – you might already – it really is a great way to get, keep and restore perspective.

All you need to do is find a special place near where you live that is your God place – the place where you go to be with the Lord. It might be a particular tree, a quiet park bench or a place near some open water. Spend a bit of time looking for this place. It needs to have a unique atmosphere and be special to you so you might not find it quickly. Then decide that you are going to go on a date with God there every so often, just to remind yourself of what it is you love about him.

During the time I was writing this book my special place to be with God was at the bottom of a field near my house. To get there you walk through a pine forest. As you turn the corner you can see the field glowing at the end of the path. You walk towards it, and it grows brighter and larger, as though you are going through a tunnel. And then you are there – at a stile, looking out across a landscape of fields and distant hills. Sitting on the stile, it is almost like you are looking out to sea, especially if the wind is blowing and the crops are whispering against each other.

I hope to be able to share everything with my husband, but I won't share this

Once you have found your place, don't tell anyone about it – just keep it a secret between you and God. I told you about mine above, because I have since moved house and I now have a new special place close to where I live. I won't tell anyone where that is. It is important to me that no-one else knows about it or shares it with me, because it is sacred to me and God.

I hope to keep finding a secret place to date God throughout my life. Even my husband, if I get one eventually, will never know where this place is. He will have to just let me go there from time to time. I hope to be able to share everything with my husband, but I won't share this. There are some things that really are between you and God, to be cherished.

I anticipate that as I grow older it will be harder to find time to get away from the rush – with all the demands of life pressing in. Maybe that will be the time to move my special place within; to my own heart. But for now it is good to be out in the open with God alone.

26

ROMANCE ADDICT?

'Life is beautiful, but sometimes I just don't know how to live it'

In the past, love in my life has tended to disappear as quickly as it arrived, like brandy burning off a Christmas pudding – and I wonder where the time went. Sometimes I think I might be a romance addict. I admonish myself to be more careful when dating. 'Don't fall too easily,' I tell myself. 'Slow down you silly girl. Don't do this to yourself again.' I am worried that if I fall so easily, each new object of affection will just come to represent freedom and an escape for the moment.

However, despite these darker moments, I am determined to keep trying and remain optimistic. Because God is love, I still believe that love is worth pursuing wholeheartedly. There is a time to guard your heart and a time to give it away. One day I believe I will give it away and get it back again tenfold.

In the past, love in my life has tended to disappear as quickly as it arrived

A little love story

Now I'd like to tell you a little love story. There is a place I sometimes sit near my house. It is a small patch of grass – a recreation area. There are two swings and a small climbing frame with a fireman's pole and a slide, two benches and two beautiful trees – one with a twisted trunk. One day during my dating time I was sitting on the climbing frame and reading the inscriptions that teenagers had carved into the wood:

'UR Gay'

(The writer was probably questioning their own orientation.)

'Janine loves the invisible man.'

(Really? Perhaps Janine is a Christian?)

'Do you like food?'

(Yes, yes I do.)

And then, a very moving one:

'Hazamandan, I sit here and all the moments come flooding back to me. Your [sic] beautiful and worth every minute of my time. I'm going 2 miss you. Mike.'

. . . then . . .

'Natalie smells of roses.'

. . . then more from Haz and Mike . . .

'To the one and only Haz. I know yr over me and don't care any more, but I really do like you so much. I think that ur incredible and mean the world to me.'

And Haz manages a reply:

'Mikey my babe. I do still care! And I adore you! Don't ever forget it because you've been my rock and will always have a special place in my heart. You're always in my thoughts too babezilla! See you soon you wonderful boy. Lots of love, Hazza.'

I was slightly scared by the use of the word 'babezilla', but fascinated by this relationship now, and quickly read on to Mike's answer:

'Haz – But I adore you as more than a friend. I know you don't believe me but you mean more to me than Rhiannon ever did . . . Ten months is a long time but I can honestly say that I think I'll like you for a long time even though you probably find that annoying. You'll never know how much you mean to me, Haz. You make me so happy with all my random happy sensations [?]. I miss you.'

There was a reply from Haz, but it was obscured by a large proclamation:

'K-Le woz ere havin raucous sex.'

Thank you, K-Le for spoiling the moment!

Anyway, for some reason this teenage romance played out across the scratched wooden walls of the climbing frame had a real poignancy. I sat there wondering what pulled Haz and Mike apart? Perhaps parental disapproval – it sounds like a cross-cultural relationship. Maybe one of them was lying to the other? Maybe Haz simply couldn't return Mike's love to the level that he loved her. We will never know the full story, as there was nothing more from either of them. I slid down the fireman's pole and headed for home, thinking about lost love.

Taking the risk

It is all very well to consider two teenagers in this context, but what about the pain of an adult relationship or a lifelong love that has come to an end?

There is an old romantic part of me that thinks it's good and right that we should leave bits of our heart in different places along life's journey. Whether a teenager's first heartbreak, or an old married couple who are finally broken apart by death, it is somehow healthy to have given your heart away. It is not only through romantic love that we part with our hearts. We leave pieces of our hearts in places we love, with far away friends, in joyful times shared with people we care about.

It is not only through romantic love that we part with our hearts

To keep our hearts to ourselves – that would be the really selfish and wrong thing. So although we may lose part of ourselves when we fall in love and it doesn't work out, or the one we love is taken from us by early death, it is a risk entirely worth taking. Indeed it is a risk we must take to be fully human and fully children of God.

We have to keep falling and trusting, succeeding and failing in love.

We also have to let ourselves heal, even with visible scars, allowing ourselves to be a little different from how we were before, ready for the next thing.

We have to ride out the storms, the doubts and difficulties and vulnerabilities. Falling in love can be wonderful and scrumptious and the most beautiful thing on earth. It can also be full of fear and vertigo and the worry of 'what if?'

So why do we all keep going? Because no matter how many times we have failed in the past, this time it might last; it might be real. This might be the one God has in store; the one to grow old with and do all the things of life with. This person might be the one to share everything with over the years – laughter, babies, holidays, worship, marriage, careers, bereavements, sex (this would come before the babies and after the marriage of course!), arguments, lazy days, busy times, boredom, quiet nights of reading or falling asleep in front of the TV, retirement parties . . . and dancing at a daughter's sixtieth birthday party in each other's arms for the final time.

I'm going to keep believing.

I hope you are too.

EPILOGUE

A question: When were you happiest in life?
An answer: Not at any one particular time, but right the way through my life, like the bubbles in champagne.

So twelve months on I have come to the end of my dating bonanza. And it has been a blast. Have I met 'the one'? I don't know. I'm not even sure that there is 'one' lined up for each of us. I have come to the understanding that no-one in this world is perfect, but that two people can learn to be perfect for each other over time.

If there's one thing I've discovered during my research, it is that life is messy and complicated. God's in there, working away – but it's sometimes hard to see how. This is true of every aspect of life, including relationships. In most cases it won't be clear-cut that he or she is 'the one' in the first few weeks or months, but sometimes you might be surprised. All you can do is follow God's leading at every step, and be willing to challenge your own pre-conceptions. I'm still doing both those things – the journey isn't over yet. Another thing I have learnt is that it's definitely more fun when you are trying.

Anyway, you've got your own story to tell and your own adventure to go on.

Finding your husband or wife is a project.

It is a quest.

It will cost you time and money.

It may cost you a little bit of dignity.

But it's so exciting.

And every time you fall down or fail it is just part of God preparing you for meeting the right person. You've got to keep trying in as many creative ways as you can. I really believe that, and it's why I wrote this book. There are so many fantastic Christians who are longing to meet someone, who feel there is no way for them to take the lead; but there is.

And every time you fall down or fail it is just part of God preparing you for meeting the right person

If you've searched your heart and prayed, and you believe that the plans God has for you include finding a husband or wife and having a family – then go out there and look. Get searching and dating. Take it seriously. Use the next twelve months and set yourself the challenge of finding dates. Even if you don't find 'the one', you will find out so much about yourself and other people – I know I did.

If you take just one thing away with you from this book, I would want it to be my discovery that *dating is a numbers game*. Very often you do have to kiss several frogs before you find your prince or princess. Some people do succeed first time, but I think it is quite rare – as rare in the Christian world as it is in the secular. Of the twenty dates that I went on, two held the promise of going somewhere or becoming anything. I think two out of twenty is a pretty good average. It could mean that once you take the decision to look for a life partner, you need to go on a maximum of ten dates before you find a suitable candidate. It might take even less time – one of my most promising dates was the second one chronologically – Simon.

Looking can take different forms as well; it is not all about the dating mechanisms I have described in this book. Though these can be helpful, another strategy is simply to make lots and lots of friends, including some of the opposite gender, without the explicit intention of finding a life partner but bearing that in mind as a possibility. The more people you know, the more likely you are to 'click' with one of them, or to be introduced to someone that you do click with.

Finally, you might groan inwardly when I say this, but I'm going to say it anyway . . . The other thing I've discovered is that actually there are a lot of things I like about being single. There is a certain joy in independence, in being able to pursue your own interests, in self-reliance and the freedom to serve God more fully. There is loneliness, but there is also excitement. Maybe I can only say that because I've been in relationships that haven't worked, but seriously – do value and cherish your life for all that it is at every stage.

Also, I have learnt this truth by observing the people around me: happiness and contentment really are to be found externally of circumstances, and no particular situation will guarantee happiness in the long-term. If you think about it, I'm pretty sure you will realize the same thing. Think for a moment about the varied levels of contentment in the people you know.

I know married people who have been together for years, are deeply happy with one another and just seem to 'fit' together. I know other married couples who are miserable, grating along, constantly sniping or backbiting. Some have a coldness between them which is worse than the fiercest arguing. I know others still who have been through harsh times or times of hating each other, and come out closer the other side; others who are always angry at each other but can't live without one another, others who are comfortable best friends without a bit of passion but with so much love . . . And the list goes on. Every couple is either happy or unhappy in their own way, and nothing guarantees happiness.

On the single side, I know people who have got to later life and are still on their own who are miserable and depressed about it, while I know others who are making the most of absolutely every opportunity to enjoy life that comes their way. Recently I have met some older people on their own who are having a fantastic time in their later years: one is planning all kinds of trips and adventures for retirement; another is surrounded by friends and relatives, always visiting or inviting people round, taking a keen interest in everyone and everything. They both seem quite content with the circumstances of their lives and have spent their time having different kinds of experiences than they might have had if they had gone down the route of getting married and having children.

Personally, after all the hard work of the intensive dating, I have come to the deep down conclusion that whatever happens in my life will happen, and so be it. I'm just going to enjoy it and make every moment as useful as I can.

100 per cent

The other thing that I have learnt is to trust – really trust.

The other thing that I have learnt is to trust – really trust

Here's a question for you that a friend asked me once (be careful – it is a trick question!): how much should you trust God in your search for a life partner and how much should you be proactive in looking for a mate?

My initial thought was 50–50. So I would be 50 per cent trusting God and 50 per cent acting on my own initiative. This seemed to make sense at first: half and half.

But thinking about it further, I realized that the only way to go is 100 per cent and 100 per cent.

You need to be 100 per cent looking and 100 per cent trusting God. You can't meander into finding the one for you – you need to be totally strategic and intentional about looking, getting to know someone and wooing them, or it isn't worth bothering. Also, you can't trust God with only half your heart; you need to really let go of the fears that you have, not cling to them. This is not always easy, I know. It took me absolutely ages to trust relationships to God 100 percent, but somehow, through all the experiences I have had, all the dates I've been on and the people I have met, I have finally reached the stage of letting go. And maybe now I'm ready? Only God knows.

For you, the journey may be at a different stage. All I can say is that if you have been out of the dating scene for a while and you want to get back into it, then I reckon you should go for it! It has been a roller-coaster ride, but the dating strategy of the last nine months writing this book has been great. It has been fun, I have learnt a lot and it has changed my attitude for the better I think. I'm sure it will be the same for you, too, if you give it a go – so go for it!

A lot of it is about your approach, and just not worrying so much! Oh yes, and if you meet someone with your new bold, light-hearted but Godly method – please do let me know – I would be delighted to hear about it!

Good luck and God bless!

Becky x

Take action – your checklist follows next page:

- Put finding a life partner on your to-do list and your prayer list today . . . right at the top!
- Commit to going on ten dates this year – or as many as it takes to find the right person.
- Look for someone in your church.
- Join a Christian dating Internet site.
- Go speed dating.
- Go to a Christian party.
- Go on a Christian holiday.
- Visit another church with friends.
- Visit another church on your own.
- Take up a new hobby.
- Go on a blind date.
- Go on a double date.
- Answer a personal ad.
- Consider whether you could go out with any of your friends.
- Be persistent – don't give up after one lousy date!
- Take things easy and keep a bit of your heart back in the early stages.
- Be brave – risk your whole heart when it feels right.
- Don't let yourself be too easily fooled by good-looks.
- Be systematic. Keep a date diary weighing up the pros and cons of each date.
- Make a seven point 'must have' list and stick to it.
- Use your head. It won't cost you your sanity if you guard your heart and do it right! In fact, it might really build your confidence (I know it's built mine).
- Kill your fantasy figure.
- Most of all, constantly ask God for guidance.
- And have fun!

Thank You

God

Mark Finnie for the original idea and sticking with it

Angela Murray for all her advice

Andy and Helen for patience and cheerfulness

Charlotte and Mareeni for unfailing friendship

Jess, Kim, Hilary, Abby, Victoria and the Rachels – girls of God, all of you!

Adrian Plass for well-placed words of encouragement

Mum and Dad for planting the seed of writing in me

All my dates for graciously letting me include them in this book – I hope you all find true and lasting love – thank you

Helen Sloane's Diary

Jeff Lucas

Take Helen, a frustrated 27-year-old rookie social worker. Add Hayley, the world's worst teenager, Kristian, the blond blue-eyed worship leader, faithful friend James, old flame Aaron, corruption, chaos and passion . . . and you've got *Helen Sloane's Diary*.

Blend in a New Age mother, a super-spiritual friend, two deeply unpleasant church members and a personal tragedy, as well as laughter, tears and thought-provoking lines and you have the recipe for a truly great story.

978-1-85078-797-6

Up Close and Personal

What Helen Did Next

Jeff Lucas

Helen Sloane, single and a social worker from Frenton-on-Sea, is struggling to rebuild her life after the murder of her father when she receives a new blow – her beloved church leaders leave. Aaron continually lets her down, James is engaged elsewhere . . . but then she meets a new man, a normal man, a wonderful man.

Has the tide turned for Helen Sloane? Will she learn the identity of her father's killer? Does hard case Hayley join the human race? Is the musical a surprise success or an embarrassing disaster? This is a heart-warming story, full of humour and insight.

978-1-85078-888-1

Distinctives

Dare To Be Different

Vaughan Roberts

In fresh and readable style Vaughan Roberts, issues a challenging call to Christians to live out their faith. We should be different from the world around us – Christian distinctives should set us apart in how we live, think, act and speak.

Targeting difficult but crucial areas such as our attitude to money and possessions, sexuality, contentment, relativism and service, this is holiness in the tradition of J.C. Ryle for the contemporary generation. Roberts helps us to consider how we are to respond biblically to the temptations and pitfalls surrounding us – giving what we cannot keep to gain what we cannot lose.

Will you take up the challenge?
Will you dare to be different?

978-1-85078-331-2

We trust you enjoyed reading this book from Authentic Media Limited. If you want to be informed of any new titles from this author and other exciting releases you can sign up to the Authentic Book Club online:

www.authenticmedia.co.uk/bookclub

Contact us
By Post: Authentic Media Limited
52 Presley Way
Crownhill
Milton Keynes
MK8 0ES

E-mail: info@authenticmedia.co.uk

Follow us: